ADVENTURES IN
NEEDLEWORK
Stitching with Passion

JESSICA ALDRED
EMILY PEACOCK

GUILD OF MASTER CRAFTSMAN PUBLICATIONS

First published 2011 by
Guild of Master Craftsman Publications Ltd
Castle Place, 166 High Street, Lewes,
East Sussex BN7 1XU

Charts and line drawings by Emily Peacock,
except for pages 120 and 140 by Jessica Aldred

ISBN 978 1 86108 895 6

A catalogue record for this book is available
from the British Library.

Publisher Jonathan Bailey
Production Manager Jim Bulley
Managing Editor Gerrie Purcell
Senior Project Editor Dominique Page
Editor Robin Pridy
Managing Art Editor Gilda Pacitti
Designer Ali Walper

Set in Gill Sans, Madfont Thorns, Lauren Script,
Rockwell and ToleCaps
Colour origination by GMC Reprographics
Printed and bound in China by Hing Yip Printing Co. Ltd.

DEDICATIONS

Emily: For Tony, Ruby and Rosa. Thank you so much for putting up with all the wool and sorry for
all those stray needles you have sat on.

Jessica: For your unfaltering support, advice and inspiration, this is for you, my mum, Wendy Aldred.

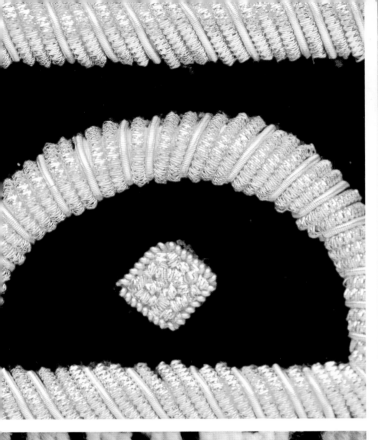
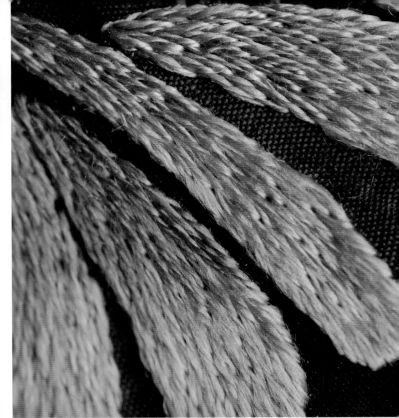

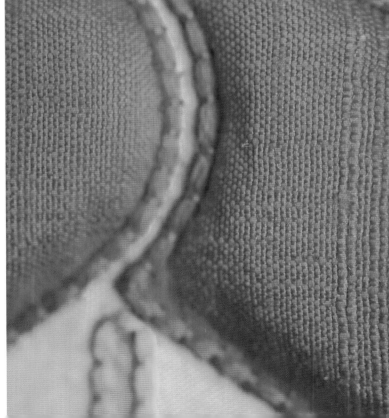

✳✳✳

CONTENTS

CHAPTER 1

CANVASWORK

CHAPTER 2

APPLIQUÉ

CHAPTER 3

SILK SHADING

CHAPTER 4

GOLDWORK

INTRODUCTION

NEEDLEWORK HAS been centre stage at the Queen's Coronation and is a regular feature at the opera and haute-couture catwalks; it has been applied to altar frontals, flags, dress and military uniforms as well as upholstery, curtains, bedding and banners. In fact, needlework has been going strong for over 20,000 years – needless to say, not long after humankind began piecing fabric together for clothing! In history, it has been not only pretty to look at but also a symbol of wealth and class and continues to play a part in each and every one of our lives.

In recent years a debate has been going on about whether embroidery is a form of art or craft. We strongly believe that it should be recognized as an art form, and this appears to be happening more and more. Hand work is time intensive and a labour of love but nothing gives you the satisfaction and sense of achievement that compare with completing a beautiful hand-stitched piece. As a medium it also has a colourful history, and many of us have our own personal memories of our grandmother's and mother's stitching – in some cases we may well remember them teaching us how to sew.

Unsurprisingly, there was a drop in the quality of hand embroidery with the invention of the sewing machine in 1830. Today, there's a huge variety of sewing machines available, many of which are computerized and allow you to input a design and let the machine do the work. To combat this automation,

organizations such as the Royal School of Needlework have stepped in, fighting to keep the art of hand embroidery alive. For our part, while we believe that every type of stitching has its place, including those from a machine, we are proud to say that the hand embroidery techniques used in this book could never be replicated using a sewing machine.

Needlework's popularity is certainly on the rise; it falls in line with the current trends for 'make do and mend' and vintage fashion. The throw-away culture of previous years has been thrown away! A wider audience is now taking an interest in needlework and more and more people – men and women – want to learn traditional techniques and spend their time and

Lonicera americana

*Top: Goldwork by **Kelley Aldridge***
*Above: Honeysuckle by **Lisa Bilby***

This is exactly what this book aims to do. We have teamed traditional techniques, many of which are used by professional embroiderers, with contemporary yet beautiful designs, in the hope that you will absolutely lose yourself in the thrill of hand embroidery. Try not to be afraid of giving anything a try. All of these projects are worked by hand – the charm is in the imperfections and so much can be learnt from trial and error. Now go for it. Adorn your homes and yourselves, make gifts for family, friends and partners, and most importantly, enjoy what you're doing.

energy creating beautiful things that will survive for future generations. And while Western culture has dictated that needlework is primarily a female pastime, history shows that it was traditionally done by men who were properly trained to master the techniques. This is still the case in countries such as India, where trained embroiderers are revered. With stitching taking on such popularity, we are seeing plenty more men taking up a needle and thread, which can only be a good thing.

Beyond its practical and aesthetic worth and its importance in history, needlework can and is being used as a remedial treatment in many different areas. Fine Cell Work is a charity that teaches needlework to prison inmates across the UK and looks to rehabilitate prisoners by giving them a chance to earn money and rebuild their lives through craft and achievement. Another organization, Bridging Arts, uses needlework to tackle difficult issues in society, reaching out to isolated communities and individuals and bringing them together through art. Its therapeutic qualities are undeniable – we can all lose ourselves in stitching, leaving our problems and worries behind.

*Top: Appliqué by **Jessica Aldred and Emily Peacock***
*Above: Elizabethan-style Sweete Bag by **Jenny Adin Christie***

***

HOW TO USE THIS BOOK

AS YOU FLIP through the book, you will see that the main body consists of four chapters, each featuring a very different yet equally exciting needlework technique for you to delve into: canvaswork, appliqué, silk shading and goldwork. To guide you through, handy sections at the beginning and end of the book provide tips, advice and basic information for those times when you need a helping hand, or perhaps just want to learn more about a particular technique.

Choose your adventure

Within a chapter, each project is designed to be a little more complicated than the previous project, with the difficulty level shown above the project title. However – this doesn't mean that you can't dip in and out as you please and have a go at any project that takes your fancy.

It may be that one particular technique inspires and excites you and that you'd like to learn as much about that technique as you possibly can. If this is the case, simply start with the first project in that chapter and work through them. Of course, it may just be that you want to start at the beginning of the book and work through every project one by one. The choice is yours...

Within each chapter

Each chapter provides an overview of the featured technique and its history, as well as brief explanations of each technique's particular uses, tools and methods. Within each project there is a list of materials and equipment, showing colours and amounts as well as providing either a chart, for canvaswork, or a photocopiable design that you can work from.

Once you have decided which project you would like to start with, treat the book a little as you might a cookery book. Read through all of the step-by-step instructions first, taking care to look at the images, and ensure you have all of the equipment and materials you need to hand.

Tricks of the trade

Throughout the book you will find 'Tricks!' These are the secrets of needlework – the things that you only pick up in classes when being taught by a professional. Learn the tricks, remember them, apply them to every project you work and tell your friends about them!

Many people would like to design their own work but feel that they don't know where to start. If you would like to make your pieces truly unique, check out the 'Make it your own!' boxes at the end of a project. These are suggestions on how to change and modify our designs to make them personal to you. Before long you will be creating original one-off pieces that are the envy of, friends, family and acquaintances alike.

Getting started

Needlework is a relatively inexpensive hobby, and the 'Materials and Equipment' section on pages 12–17 should provide you with all the information on what you will need. Start by collecting the items to form your basic kit, and your collection of specialist equipment, fabrics and threads will grow over time as you progress through different projects.

Preparatory techniques, including how to transfer a design, start and finish threads and prepare your frame ready to start working, is covered in the 'Basic Techniques' section on pages 18–25. If at any point you are unsure of how to do a stitch, be sure to check out the 'Stitch Glossary' on pages 26–29.

Sewing it all up

Once you have finished your actual needlework design, you may want to turn it into something, such as a cushion, a wall hanging or even mount it in a very special frame. The 'Finishing Techniques' section on pages 152–160 explains how to do this.

The end of the book features a list of useful reading, including books that might further inspire, inform and teach, plus a list of suppliers that tells you where we have purchased everything. Of course, feel free to shop around, as there are plenty of fantastic materials and equipment available.

A little advice

The practice of making anything requires a particular mindset. A common question we are always asked by those beginning to take up needlework is 'How long will it take me?' As you will discover (and as many embroiderers and stitchers can already testify to), the creation process brings great joy and satisfaction and it is not simply about the completion of a project. As two devoted needleworkers we have both discovered the immense pleasure needlework offers. In as much as a walk is taken to enjoy the scenery and a meal is enjoyed through its taste, smell and sight, needlework is also a sensory pleasure.

In this book you will begin to understand and enjoy watching the subtle blending and taking shape of silk threads; the drama of contrast, stitching one fabric upon another to create strong graphic shapes; bringing together small, delicate fragments of metal to build a dazzling texture; and working in a more uniform and structured way as small, plump stitches of wool lie together to build a beautiful design.

And so begins your Adventures in Needlework…

MATERIALS AND EQUIPMENT

NEEDLEWORK DOESN'T HAVE to be an expensive hobby. To start with, simply invest in the basic kit items listed on page 15, all of which can be bought quite cheaply. Then, once you have a few projects under your belt you can start to build up your collection of the more specialized equipment. Your stash of fabric, threads and embellishments will also grow as you go along.

Most of the needlework equipment listed here has been used for centuries and is ideal to help you achieve the traditional techniques used in this book. In fact, antique needlework tools are highly collectable, although if it interests you, you may be able to find some at reasonable prices on auction websites, at auction or in antique shops.

Materials
• •

A bit of fabric, some thread or wool, perhaps a ribbon or a few beads – with the right tools and willing hands, they can become truly beautiful works of art. Here are a few descriptions of what we've used in the book.

FABRIC

In this book we have primarily used silks and cottons in a variety of different colours and weights for both the appliqué and silk shading projects. Do be aware, however, that you may need to attach light fabrics on to a backing fabric (such as calico) in order to give it

strength. The metal threads in the goldwork section can also be worked on any type of fabric – we've used cotton, linen and velvet, but you can choose any fabric you wish.

For canvaswork, a tapestry or needlwork canvas is used and is referred to by its 'count'. This is the number of holes per inch or centimetre. The higher the 'count', the finer the wool and the more delicate the work. A lower count has wider holes, which uses thicker wool and gives a coarser, but no less attractive, finish. Canvas comes in many forms – rug canvas, plastic canvas, 'Penelope' canvas, mono canvas or mono interlock canvas. The projects in this book use the latter, as it is both easy to manipulate and securely woven.

TRICK! Where possible, always try to use natural fabrics as they are usually of a better quality than artificial fibres. In this book you will see that we have used a variety of types, weights and colours of fabrics.

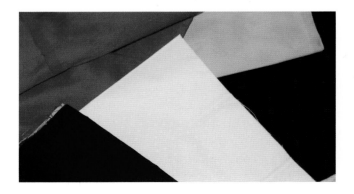

use machine threads to sew down the padding and to couch over or secure down a variety of metal threads.

TRICK! Our advice is to keep your thread lengths short – no longer than the distance between your wrist and elbow. This helps you get into the rhythm of stitching, keeps the threads clean and avoids them wearing down. Remember to always have a good sharp pair of embroidery scissors to hand.

THREADS

From cotton, silk and wool to gold, silver and copper, there is a thread to suit any technique in needlework. There are all sorts of threads available – variegated cottons and wools in candy colours, luxurious silks and machine threads in jewel brights.

The canvaswork projects use 100 per cent pure virgin wool created using the worsted technique. This refers to a common method of producing yarns suitable for being pulled through a canvas, as the fibres that make up the yarn are long and lie parallel to each other. A fine crewel wool (also known as '2 ply') is used two strands thick for a finely woven canvas, while a tapestry wool (4 ply) worked in a single strand is best for a slightly wider woven canvas.

For appliqué, we have used machine threads to secure down the fabrics and stranded cottons to decorate, as machine threads are strong and hard wearing, and stranded cottons can be separated, enabling you to vary the thickness of the stitch as desired. Silk shading can be done in silk threads or stranded cottons. For goldwork

EMBELLISHMENTS

Some of our projects incorporate embellishments such as beads, sequins and crystals. There are a huge amount of these available, from the reassuringly inexpensive to those that drip with jaw-dropping luxury. Shop around – check out your local haberdashery shop or department, buy job lots at online auctions and go mad in specialist shops such as those listed on our 'Suppliers' pages at the end of the book. We've used a selection of drop beads, hot fix crystals and sequins, but you don't have to stick with our suggestions – choose whatever you like.

Equipment

Even with your basic kit (see opposite), it is important to understand that each of these four types of needlework will work best with differing sets of materials and equipment – some use a frame, some don't. Canvaswork uses, well, canvas! And while appliqué can use even the flimsiest silk, this would not work so well for the dense stitching of silk shading.

CANVASWORK

This is probably one of the simplest forms of needlework in terms of materials and equipment – you really only need wool, a tapestry needle and a woven canvas, and you are away!

Wool is a very user-friendly, natural material. The softness of wool ensures that imperfections do not show up and canvaswork projects are very easy to pick up and put down. These aspects of canvaswork make it a great hobby for those starting to explore the world of needlework, and will help build confidence.

Using wool is not dissimilar to painting onto a canvas. Wools come in a variety of shades and can be used in very graphic designs, but can also be used for more subtle shading. For more information on the specifics of wool and canvas, see pages 12–13.

Of course, there are a few additional things you can add to your canvaswork kit. You can use a tapestry frame if you want, or you can simply use masking tape to bind the canvas. And if you choose, you can use a marker to pinpoint where each wool colour should go when using a chart. For more information on this and on using a frame, see 'Basic Techniques', pages 22–25.

APPLIQUÉ

For this type of needlework, you can be as austere or as lavish as you like with your fabrics, threads and embellishments. Use whatever takes your fancy – cottons, velvet and silks, stripes, dots and patterns – put them all together! Decorate with stranded cotton and Japanese thread, sequins and beads, crystals and ribbons. With appliqué, anything goes! This technique is also very tactile, and the best way to add dimension is to use felt overlaid with fabric – you will see in our projects how these padded areas 'rise' up above the rest of the design to stunning effect.

All the appliqué projects in this book require you to transfer a photocopiable design onto fabric. For this, a light box and a quilter's pencil come in handy, but are not essential – see 'Basic Techniques' on pages 18–20 for more on design transfer. Also, with all this layering of fabric comes the need to press, so if you're planning on doing a lot of appliqué, an iron would make a good investment.

SILK SHADING

The star of the show for silk shading is, of course, the thread. Traditionally silk, the thread used nowadays for this technique is mostly stranded cottons. These are less slippy and a little thicker, so it takes less time to cover an area. However, silks have a more luxurious quality and if you want to use these for the projects within the book, they will work beautifully.

Although less apparent, it is equally important to choose an appropriate backing fabric in silk shading. You can stitch directly on to heavy silks and cottons but if you choose a medium to lightweight fabric you may need to apply it to a second backing – cotton calico is preferred – to give it extra strength. With such dense stitching, there is a risk of tearing if you were working

Embroidery scissors (Ⓐ) Make sure you have a good pair of sharp embroidery scissors. Buy a cheap but sharp pair specifically for cutting metal threads, as they soon become blunt.

Fabric scissors (Ⓑ) Invest in a good pair of fabric scissors and don't be tempted to use them for anything else!

Frames (Ⓒ) If you're looking to keep costs down, use a ring frame for any of the projects or you can use masking tape to bind the edges for the canvaswork. See 'Basic Techniques' on pages 22–25 for more on this, as well as to read about the more specialized slate, clip and tapestry frames.

Iron (Ⓓ) A regular iron is absolutely fine – just make sure the plate is clean before ironing your fabrics. In some cases, particularly for appliqué, a mini iron is useful, although not essential.

Needles (Ⓔ) Canvaswork uses tapestry needles, which have a blunt end that inserts easily between the twists of each thread rather than splitting them, while the rest of the techniques use regular sewing needles, usually straight. We haven't specified exactly what size needles to use in the projects – it is best to keep a variety of sizes and use the smallest needles you feel comfortable with without spending hours struggling to thread your needle.

Paper scissors (Ⓕ) This is for the projects that require you to cut out shapes from the paper design.

Pins (Ⓖ) Always have some good-quality glass-headed pins to hand, both for the project designs themselves and for the finishing techniques.

Screwdriver, small (Ⓗ) This is essential for tightening up your ring frames; those that come with sewing machines are usually quite small and good for this job.

Tape measure (Ⓘ) Another necessary piece of equipment, your tape measure should have both metric and imperial measurements on it.

directly on to a medium or lightweight fabric. If you're not sure whether to back your fabric, do a little tester to see if it will stand the density of your stitching. There are several ways to transfer the photocopiable design in silk shading – you can use a light box or a window, or you can 'prick and pounce'. Pricking and pouncing requires special materials and equipment, as listed. (See 'Basic Techniques' on pages 18–25.)

Charcoal (A) Ground down to a powder, this makes black pounce, which is used in the 'pricking, pouncing and painting' method of transferring a design.

Coloured pencils (B) Used for doing coloured shadings for silk shading, these can also be used for transferring on designs.

Cuttlefish Ground down to a powder, this makes white pounce, which is used in the 'pricking, pouncing and painting' method of transferring a design.

Light box (C) Used for transferring designs, this isn't an essential piece of equipment, as taping your design on to a window works just as well (it just isn't quite so comfortable).

Pricker (D) Also known as a 'pin vice', this is a tool that holds a needle in the end of it for the 'pricking, pouncing and painting' method of transferring a design.

Tracing paper (E) Always have some good-quality tracing paper to hand.

Watercolour paints Used for transferring a design in the 'pricking, pouncing and painting' method, and to paint backgrounds on occasion. Buy in tubes rather than blocks.

Quilter's pencil (F) These pencils have special leads that don't smudge when you run your hand over them – perfect for transferring designs on to fabric.

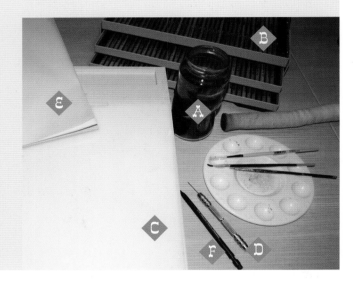

GOLDWORK

This technique actually uses all types of metal threads, of which there are two main types: those that have a cotton core with a metallic foil wrapped around it, and those that are made of metal wire.

If you want to use gold threads, it may come as a surprise to learn that not all gold threads will have a content of real gold. Gold threads are better quality, but if you want to keep costs down, choose gilt threads, which have no real gold content.

You will need a small block of beeswax for goldwork, as waxing the threads avoids them breaking if they rub against jagged ends. It also improves your tension, giving the thread more grip. You may also want to invest in some specialist tools for this technique – a mellor and a stiletto can be particularly useful (see opposite for details of specialist equipment).

Beeswax (A) Used for waxing the threads in gold work, this gives the threads more grip and stops them from catching and breaking on sharp ends of the metal threads.

Bracing needle (B) Used for framing up a slate frame.

Clamping tools These are small metal bars with an indentation at one end, used to fasten the clasps around flat back crystals, so that they lie in a setting.

Curved needle (C) You may find it more comfortable to use a curved needle for slip stitching, which is useful for appliqué and when mounting your projects.

Fabric glue This is handy for finishing techniques such as mounting something to frame. It is very strong and clear. The glue is flexible when dried so can move with the project rather than forming a rigid bond that could crack.

Iron-on adhesive This has paper on one side – you iron it on to your fabric, peel off the paper, place another piece of fabric on top and iron the two together. It's particularly useful for appliqué projects.

Masking tape Used to bind the edges of your canvas while working, to stop it from fraying.

Mellor (D) Also known as a 'laying tool', a mellor is useful but not essential for goldwork, as you can use it to lay and manipulate the threads rather than touch them with your hands (the oils in your skin can cause damage to metal threads).

Paper-covered wire (E) Used more often for cake decorating, it can also be used in embroidery to create raised work, as seen in our Goldwork chapter.

Sewing machine 'Oh no', you cry! Yes, even in the world of hand stitching, a sewing machine can be useful and speedy, particularly for making curtains and the unseen parts of other finishing techniques.

Stiletto (F) A pointy tool for making holes, this is useful in gold work for making holes in your fabric through which you plunge the ends of your metal threads.

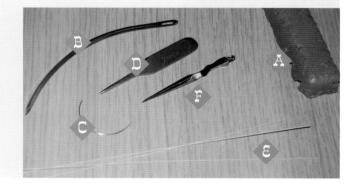

Make it your own!

This list is not exhaustive, the world is your oyster and there are many excellent retailers out there. When searching for fabrics, threads and embellishments use your imagination, and don't be afraid to make it your own!

* * *

BASIC TECHNIQUES

THIS SECTION TELLS YOU everything you need to know about getting started; the all-important preparation before you begin stitching.

Transferring a design

There are various ways you can transfer a design on to fabric and choosing the right one simply depends on the size of your project, the thickness of your fabric and the nature of the technique. The traditional way of transferring a design is by 'pricking, pouncing and painting' the design on to the fabric but this can be a lengthy process.

Where possible it's absolutely fine to draw on designs with pencil (a quilter's pencil is best for this as the lines don't smudge), using a light box or a window. If working from a chart, you can map out the design with a fine permanent marker if you need to.

USING A LIGHT BOX

If you plan on doing plenty of embroidery, a light box (also known as a light tracer) can be extremely useful. To save money, you can try to find a secondhand one using an online auction.

To use a light box, first lay your design on the box and then lay your fabric over top of the design. You can secure them both with a bit of masking tape so that they don't shift while you draw on your design with a quilter's pencil (**A**).

If you do not wish to buy a light box, you can, of course, use the big light in the sky! Tape your design on to a window, tape your fabric over the top and draw your design on with a quilter's pencil. This isn't as comfortable as using a light box, but is equally effective. (**B**)

PRICKING, POUNCING AND PAINTING

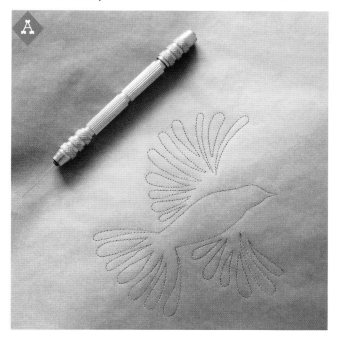

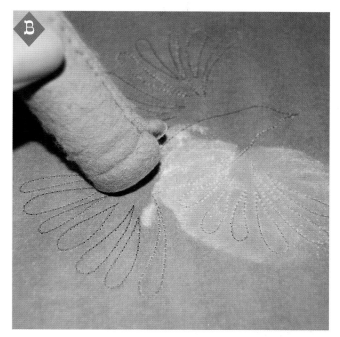

This is the traditional way of transferring a design on to fabric and it's necessary to do when the fabric is too thick to see the design through on a light box or using a window.

1 Trace the design on to a piece of tracing paper.

2 Prick holes along all of the design lines, around 1/12in (2mm) apart. To do this you can use a pricker or a 'pin vice', a little tool which grasps a needle or pin at one end of so that you can hold it like a pencil (see 'Materials and Equipment', page 16). If you don't have a pricker, just hold the needle as best you can while you prick the holes (lay the tracing paper on a spare or unused cushion while you prick the holes) (**A**).

3 For the next step you need to get yourself some pounce. Pounce is either ground-down charcoal (for black), cuttlefish bone (for white) or a mixture of both for grey. You will need to grind your own in a pestle and mortar, as it's not sold anywhere as pounce. If you don't quite fancy the idea of grinding down cuttlefish bone, use white chalk pastels instead. If possible, put your fabric in your frame before transferring the design. Lay your pricking on to your fabric and position the design as central as you can. Using a rolled-up thick cotton or felt cloth, dab the end in the pounce and then, still using the rolled-up end of your cloth, rub in circular motions over the design (**B**).

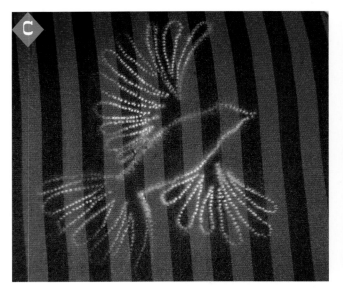

4 Lift off your pricking carefully and, if you need to, you can gently blow off any excess pounce. If you can't see the design clearly or the powder has shifted, simply blow it all off and start again. Now your design should be on the fabric in tiny dots of powder. (**C**).

5 For the last stage, painting on, use watercolour paint (choose the paint that comes in tubes rather than blocks) and pick a colour, or a mixture of colours, that are sympathetic to the colour scheme of your project, just in case any of the design lines are visible at the end.

6 Using a fine paint brush, carefully paint on the lines, being careful not to disturb any of the pounce (don't sneeze!) as you go – work from right to left if you are right-handed and the other way if you are left-handed to avoid this. Once the whole of the design is painted on, leave it to dry and then blow away any of the leftover pounce – banging the back of your work also gets rid of this (**D**).

USING A CHART

All the canvaswork projects in this book use charts, which are basically maps that indicate where stitches are placed. You will find these at the beginning of each project, along with a symbol key.

For cross stitch and tent stitch, each square on the chart represents one stitch worked over one intersection of canvas. Colours and symbols are used to represent different colour threads. For Bargello work, each square on the chart represents one canvas thread to be stitched over vertically.

Starting and finishing threads

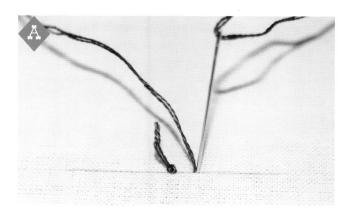

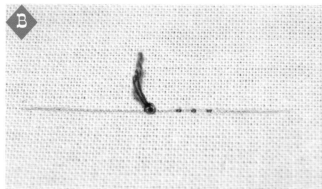

1 Put a knot in the end of your thread and take the needle down through your fabric, within the design, leaving the knot on the top (**A**).

2 Do three tiny stitches to secure your thread, then bring the needle back up through the fabric and cut off the knot (not shown). As you work over them, your thread will be secured by those little stitches. This is called the waste knot technique and means there won't be any knots on the back and you don't need to keep turning your frame over (**B**).

3 To finish your thread again, do a few little stitches within your design, bring your needle up to the top and cut off the thread (**C**).

4 For the canvaswork projects, use the same technique, but instead of doing the holding stitches in step 2, simply leave the knot on the top of the fabric, bring your thread up 1½in (4cm) away from the knot and continue working. Once the long thread on the back has been caught in by your stitches, cut the knot off.

TRICK! If you don't have any space within the design to finish your thread, or if you are working on canvas, simply turn your work over and weave your thread through the stitches on the back.

Frames

There are many different types of embroidery frames available and it's easy to get confused as to which one will work best for the result you'd like to achieve. Listed below are the different types of frames we've used for the projects in this book, but if you find a particular frame you're comfortable working with, feel free to stick with it.

RING FRAMES

Ring frames are perfect for small projects. Where you can, always use a ring frame with a dowel so that it can be attached to either a seat stand or barrel clamp, leaving both of your hands free to work.

It's a good idea to stick with three sizes of ring frames: 6, 8 and 10in (15, 20 and 25cm). Bind your ring frames with strips of calico or fabric tape to ensure your fabric stays taught and doesn't get marked by the wood. To do this, simply put double-sided sticky tape around both the inside and outside frames and wrap the fabric/tape around, securing at the end with a few stitches. It's really important to keep your fabric as tight as possible in the frame as this avoids puckering later on.

Ring frames are used for the following projects: One, Bleeding Rose, Winged Brooch, Ferris Wheel, Golden Apple, Kissing Couple and Bird in Flight.

WOODEN TAPESTRY FRAMES

Traditional tapestry or hand-rotating frames are perfect for canvaswork. Frames are available in a variety of widths and you should choose one that easily houses the width of your cut canvas.

The frames typically have two fixed side bars 12in (30cm) long and two rotating horizontal bars top and bottom with a strip of webbing running along them. The cut top and bottom edges of your canvas should be stitched to this webbing and then the surplus rolled over the bars until the desired tension is reached. Wooden tapestry frames are sold as hand-held, on a floor stand or even attached to a beanbag for your lap.

> TRICK! If you prefer not to use a frame (for designs using cross stitch, for example), you may find that folding long strips of masking tape around the outside of the cut canvas is a great way to prevent the wool (or your clothes!) catching on the raw edges.

CLIP FRAMES

For appliqué projects that are too big for your ring frames, clip frames are perfect, as the fabric doesn't need to be super tight in the frame for this technique.

These are super easy to use. You simply cut the width of your fabric to fit the frame, roll your fabric on to both ends of the frame, attach the arms and attach the clips.

The Rabbit in a Top Hat project uses a clip frame.

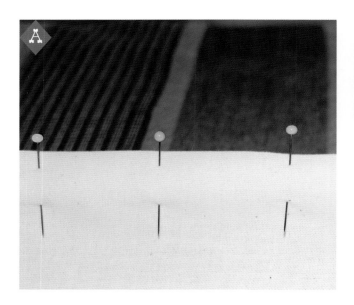

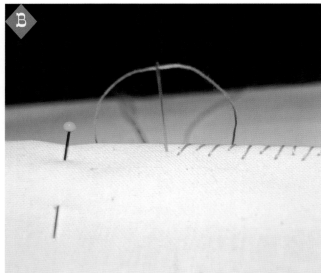

SLATE FRAMES

For larger projects where the fabric does need to be under tension, nothing beats a slate frame. Slate frames can be costly and take time to prepare, but if you want to do large projects or a lot of embroidery, it is really worth investing in one.

Using a slate frame is a little more involved, but lots of people say that once they've used one they don't want to use any other type of frame! Here's how you frame up with a slate frame:

1 On the bars of the frame, mark the centre of the webbing with a pencil. Fold a ½in (12mm) turning at the top and bottom of your fabric then fold it in half to find the centre. Match this up with your marking, and pin in place (◆A◆). Working outwards, pin your fabric all the way along the webbing.

2 Stitch in place using a buttonhole thread and, again, work from the centre outwards. Alternate the stitches so some are long and some shorter. This stops the webbing from tearing when you come to tighten up your frame later (◆B◆).

3 Fasten off your thread by stitching back over your stitches a few times (◆C◆).

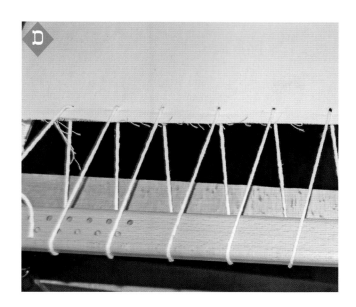

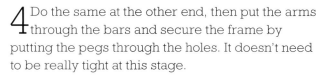

4 Do the same at the other end, then put the arms through the bars and secure the frame by putting the pegs through the holes. It doesn't need to be really tight at this stage.

5 To avoid the fabric tearing you can stitch a length of webbing down each side of your fabric using the buttonhole thread.

6 Using a bracing needle, string the webbing to the arms of the frame, leaving the two ends loose. Always stitch down in to the webbing rather than up through it (**D**).

7 Tighten up the frame. The best way to do this is to put the frame on the floor, push the bar down with your foot and move the peg to the lowest hole that you can get it in – you may need someone to help you with this! (**E**)

8 Finally, tighten up the string, and secure at the end with a knot.

The Drama project uses a slate frame.

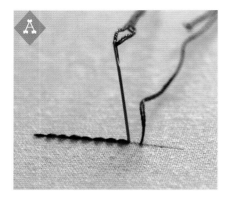

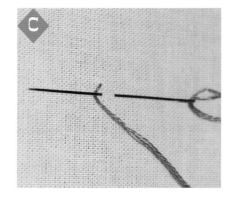

***

STITCH GLOSSARY

NEVER FEAR, HELP IS HERE! Use this handy guide if you become confused about a stitch, or feel you need to know just a little bit more to become confident about using a particular stitch.

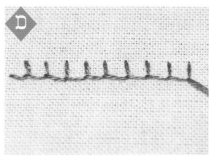

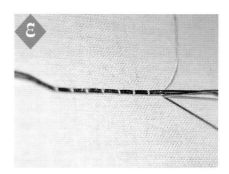

BACK STITCH

Simply bring the needle up through the fabric and take it down at the end of the previous stitch (**A**).

BRICKING

When couching (see right) over threads, it is advisable to brick your stitches. This means that the stitches from your second row onwards should sit between and at right angles to those of the previous row (**B**).

BUTTONHOLE STITCH

Put the needle through the fabric, hold the thread on the top and bring the needle up within the loop of the thread (**C**)(**D**).

COUCHING

This technique involves stitching over the thread or threads that you have already simply laid down on the top of your chosen fabric, to secure it down. It is sometimes used to provide an outline covering a raw edge of fabric that has been applied to another piece of fabric (**E**).

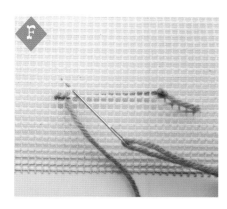

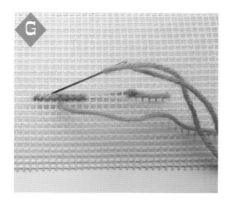

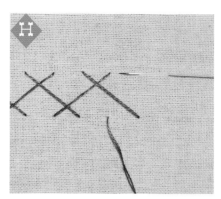

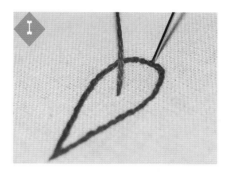

CROSS STITCH

This can be done in one of two ways. Firstly, bring your needle from the back of your work to the front and take it down into the hole that lies diagonally above it. This is a half cross stitch. Now bring your needle up again through the hole directly underneath and bring your needle up diagonally, parallel to your last stitch. Continue in this way until you have reached the end of the row, then return and cross all the stitches (**F**) (**G**). Alternatively you can form the crosses as you go.

CUTWORK

This technique is used in gold work. First cut the hollow metal threads down to the size you wish them to be, then bring the needle up through your fabric. Thread on the gold then take the needle down through the fabric, thus stitching the piece down as you would a bead.

HERRINGBONE STITCH

This stitch is used when mounting a completed project ready for framing. Slip the needle through the fabric, then just above this, cross the thread over your previous stitch and slip the needle through the fabric again (**H**).

LONG AND SHORT STITCH

A misleading name! This is the stitch that is used in silk shading. Despite the name, your stitches shouldn't be of regimented lengths. Think of it as long and long, or long and little bit shorter! (**I**)(**J**)(**K**).

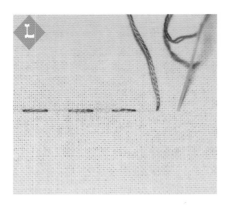

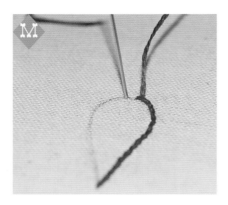

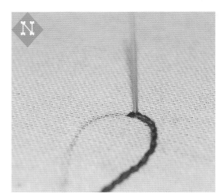

RUNNING STITCH

One of the most basic, yet still very effective stitches. Bring your needle up through the fabric, taking it back down the distance away that you want your stitch length to be. Leaving the same sized gap, bring your needle up and carry on in this way, thus creating a line of straight stitches with gaps in between (**L**).

SLIP STITCH

This stitch is used when sewing two pieces of fabric together on which you have folded the fabric under like a hem. A curved needle can be useful for slip stitching.

SPLIT STITCH

Used to create clean, neat edges in silk shading, simply do a tiny stitch and bring the needle up in the thread of your previous stitch. (**M**)(**N**).

STAB STITCH

This stitch is used when sewing one piece of fabric on top of another. Bring the needle up on the outside edge and take it down into the fabric that is being applied (**O**)(**P**).

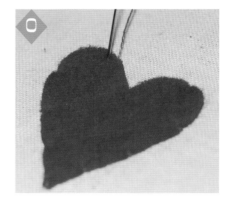

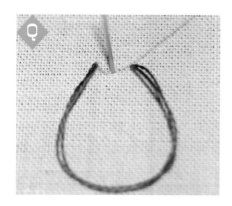

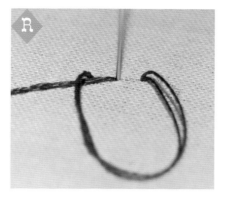

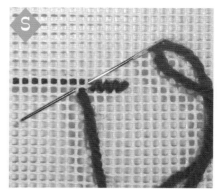

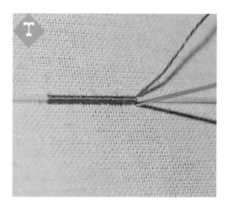

STEM STITCH

This is a great stitch for doing outlines. Bring the needle up, take it down while holding a loop of the thread on the top of the fabric and bring your needle up again in the middle of where you originally came up and went down. From your second stitch onwards, bring your needle up at the end of your previous stitch (Q)(R).

TRAILING

This is a form of couching where the stitches are more tightly packed together. It is excellent for lettering or trailing over cake wire to create three-dimensional forms, which is also known as stump work. (T).

TENT STITCH

Start at the top of a row by bringing your needle up and then down into the hole that lies diagonally to the left of your work as you look at it. Bring the needle up again into the hole that lies to the right of your initial starting place and down diagonally to the left, so that it lies parallel to your first stitch. Continue in this way, creating small diagonal stitches that on the surface look like a half cross stitch but have a padded reverse side (S).

canvaswork

1

CANVASWORK

THE DURABLE NATURE OF CANVASWORK HAS ALWAYS MADE IT PERFECT FOR INTERIORS, WHERE IT HAS BEEN USED TO ADORN WALLS, BEDS AND EVEN UPHOLSTERY. NOWADAYS, ITS RENEWED POPULARITY SEES IT ON EVERYTHING FROM CUSHIONS TO HANDBAGS.

IT WAS THE VICTORIAN craze for Berlin woolwork that first brought canvaswork to the fore. Its charted designs, worked in single canvas in tent and cross stitches, included depictions of plants, flowers and animals and were very much the height of fashion. However, with this fad came a lack of individuality and Berlin woolwork went just as quickly out of fashion in the 1870s.

Yet working in wool and canvas – sometimes known as needlepoint, or tapestry, even though tapestry traditionally refers to a woven textile – has always been a popular form of embroidery. Designs are created primarily through colour using simple stitches such as cross stitch or tent stitch, although the type the technique known as Bargello, which uses long vertical stitches of varying length, can also give a texture to your work.

You will notice that canvas is referred to by count. It is available in a very fine mesh of 24 holes to the inch (tpi) or an open weave of 5 holes to the inch. The finer the mesh, the more detailed the work. Very fine needlepoint worked in tent stitch on 24 tpi is called 'petit point' but most commercial needlepoint kits use a count of 10, 12 or 14. Canvas is also available in single-thread and double-thread forms and can be worked on with many different threads, including silk or cotton. Traditionally, however, canvaswork is associated with using a woollen yarn.

Opposite: Canvas shading by **Sophie Long**
Above: Jekyll Iris Kit c/o **Royal School of Needlework**
Top right: Sweete Bag detail by **Jenny Adin Christie**

If you are not using a frame and you find the canvas initially quite stiff to work with, do not be afraid to manipulate it with your hands to soften it. Any creases can be worked out at the 'blocking' stage after the work is completed.

THE PROJECTS

The five projects in this chapter illustrate the diversity that canvaswork offers and we hope they will inspire you. Our *Fish Tattoo* bag illustrates perfectly how canvaswork can create beautiful three-dimensional pieces. The palette of colours in the projects varies from the more muted, Old West tones of *Lean on Me*, through to the bright flames and coloured crystals of *Passion*. *Bargello Sardines* offers an opportunity for you to experiment with your own bold colours to create an edgy retro feel, and *Love is in the Air* may be for the more romantically inclined!

Lean on Me

IT'S GREAT FUN TO USE LETTERING IN A DESIGN, AND THIS IS CERTAINLY THE
PERFECT PHRASE FOR A CUSHION THAT DEMANDS YOUR FULL ATTENTION.

THIS DESIGN is inspired by the nostalgic yet edgy woodblock fonts seen on saloon doors or posters in the American Old West. The earthy colours and stars-and-arrows motif add to the cushion's homely, romantic feel. This pillow would make a great gift, if you can bear to part with it...

The needlework is not at all difficult, and the design is worked in counted **cross stitch** from the colour chart provided. To see how to do this, go to the 'Stitch Glossary' on page 27.

Finished size of design: approx. 19 x 17in (48 x 43cm).

Materials

Mono interlock canvas,
10 holes per inch
25 x 23in (64 x 59cm) minimum

Appleton Bros crewel wool
(available in skeins of 27yd
(25m) or hanks of 197yd
(180m):

White 991 • 263yd (240m)

Autumn Yellow 472
241yd (220m)

Honeysuckle Yellow 692
175yd (160m)

Brown Groundings 582
121yd (110m)

Dull Marine Blue 323
88yd (80m)

Turquoise 521 • 71yd (65m)

Flame Red 208 • 33yd (30m)

Autumn Yellow 474
22yd (20m)

Golden Brown 901
14yd (12m)

Equipment

Size 20 tapestry needle

Masking tape

Permanent marker

KEY

+ White 991	≡ Brown Groundings 582	% Flame Red 208
~ Autumn Yellow 472	ꓥ Dull Marine Blue 323	: Autumn Yellow 474
< Honeysuckle Yellow 692	# Turquoise 521	O Golden Brown 901

Instructions

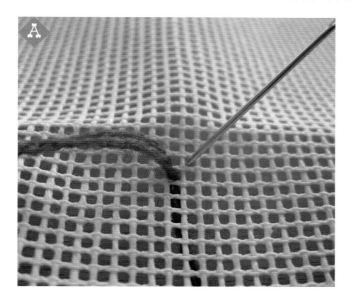

1 Bind the edges of the canvas with masking tape as described in 'Basic Techniques' on page 23. Now fold the canvas in half and then in half again – this determines the centre of the design as indicated on the chart.

2 You can either begin at, or near, this centre point, or measure 3in (7.5cm) in from the sides and begin at the edge of the chart.

3 Fold the crewel wool in half and thread it through the needle, leaving the looped end longer than the cut end. Secure the first stitch by pulling the wool through the canvas from the back to the front, leaving the looped end hanging, then stitching the first diagonal of the cross stitch (◆A).

4 Secure the wool by passing it through the loop at the back of the work (◆B).

5 Begin by cross stitching those parts of the design nearest to your starting place, in this case, at the centre point, with the word 'on' (C) (D).

TRICK! Use a permanent marker of a similar colour to your wool and use it as a guide. Indicate the position of the stitches by marking a small dot in the cross point of each stitch. This can speed up the process of having to refer to the chart for each row.

6 To finish a thread, run your needle through the back of the completed stitches and do a 'loop the loop', returning a couple of stitches back, but keeping the needle in the same direction (E). Trim the thread.

7 Continue to cross stitch the word 'on' in the Flame Red colour (F) before outlining the letters in white as indicated on the chart.

TRICK! These steps work in a logical progression, filling in the background after the lettering and design elements have been worked. You may prefer to work some of the background as you go, so that it does not feel too monotonous at the end!

8 Work the shadowed outline of 'LEAN' and 'ME' in Brown Groundlings, beginning with those letters nearest to your starting place (◆G◆). Continue stitching until all the letters are outlined (◆H◆).

9 Now you can begin to stitch a white keyline on the inside border of the shadowed letters before filling in the central portion with the two shades of blue. You can either do the keyline and filling one letter at a time, or do the keyline for all the letters before blocking in the blues throughout (◆I◆).

10 Once you have finished stitching one letter, or perhaps all of them, you can start to work the Golden Brown and Flame Red colours of the horizontals in the letters (J), until all the letters are complete (K).

11 With the letters finished, fill the separate design elements – the arrows and the stars – as well as stitch the cushion's inner border (L).

12 First stitch the dividing lines of the 'rays' before filling them in with the two different tones of yellow (◆M◆). Now you can finish the design by working the outer border in white (◆N◆).

Your design is now ready to stretch and frame or make into a cushion, as shown in 'Finishing Techniques' on page 152–156.

Make it your own!

Give this cushion your own stamp with your choice of trimming. Look for trimmings that compliment the theme, such as twisted leather and suede or rope-effect cords.

Bargello Sardines

THIS RETRO SARDINES CUSHION IS PERFECT FOR USING UP ODDS AND ENDS OF TAPESTRY WOOL AND IT GIVES YOU A CHANCE TO REALLY EXPERIMENT WITH COLOUR – THE END RESULT IS COOL, QUIRKY AND CHIC.

BARGELLO IS A CANVAS work technique using long vertical stitches in repeated wave or flame formations. It relies heavily on colour and shading to create a striking effect. It is not difficult and can be very quick to do. Refer to the chart provided, but be as bold as you like with colour – the more contrast you mix into the design, the more retro it will look.

This design is a modern take on a traditional stitch – but the key thing to note is that the fish scales run from light to dark on both the body and head, '1' being the lightest and '5' being the darkest on the body, 'A' being the lightest and 'E' being the darkest on the head.

Finished size of design: approx. 19 x 17in (48 x 43cm).

Materials

**Mono interlock canvas
14 holes per inch**
25 x 17in (64 x 43cm) minimum

**Medium-weight cotton
backing fabric**
Cut to the size of the canvas

**Machine thread to match
background colour** • 1 spool

**Four-hole buttons, approx.
1¼in (3cm) round** • 3

**Tapestry wool in the
following amounts (available
in skeins of 27yd (25m) or
hanks of 197yd (180m):**

Sardine heads
Cream • 14¼ yd (13m)
Lime green • 15⅓ yd (14m)
Turquoise • 14¼ yd (13m)
Blue • 11yd (10m)
Darkest blue • 18½ yd (17m)

Sardine bodies
White • 16½ yd (15m)
Palest grey • 15⅓ yd (14m)
Mid grey • 12yd (11m)
Dark grey • 7¾ yd (7m)
Darkest grey • 13¼ yd (12m)

Tin interior
Red • 36yd (33m)

Tin edge
Yellow • 5½ yd (5m)

Background
Orange • 45yd (41m)

Sardine mouth
Pink • 2¼ yd (2m)

Equipment

Size 20 tapestry needle
Masking tape

COLOUR PHOTOCOPY
AT 180%

KEY

- `1` Cream
- `2` Lime green
- `3` Turquoise
- `4` Blue
- `5` Darkest blue

- `A` White
- `B` Palest grey
- `C` Mid grey
- `D` Dark grey
- `E` Darkest grey

- `≡` Red
- `%` Yellow
- `□` Orange
- `+` Pink

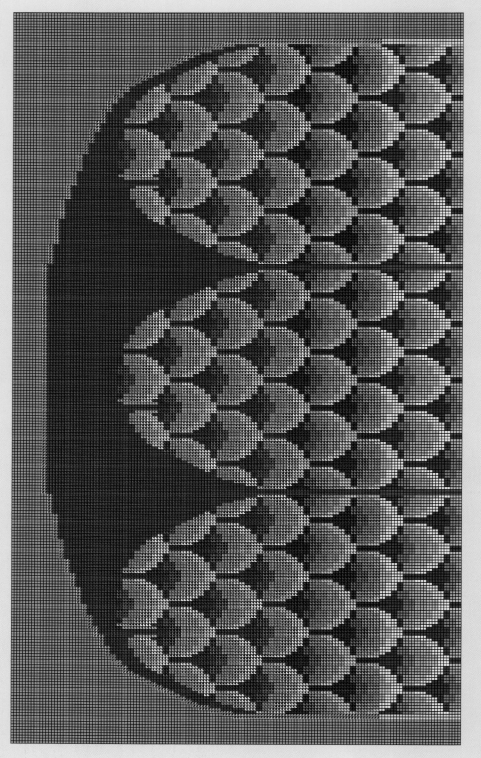

ADVENTURES IN NEEDLEWORK

Instructions

  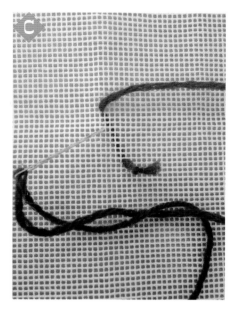

1 Bind the edges of the canvas with masking tape, as described in 'Basic Techniques' on page 23.

2 Beginning with the sardine scales, note that they are made from vertical stitches worked over four or two threads. Each square represents wool passed over a thread of canvas, so a vertical line of four coloured squares would mean you pass the needle though a hole in the canvas and then up (or down) over four threads of canvas. See the stitched 'scale' (Ⓐ) and chart detail (Ⓑ) to see how the areas of colour are broken down.

3 Measure in 3in (10cm) from the centre bottom edge of your canvas and start to work colour '5' of the sardine bodies. Tie a knot at one end of the wool and insert the needle from front to back a few stitches away from where you will stitch, in the direction in which you are stitching (Ⓒ). Once you reach the knot, snip it off close to the canvas – this is the canvas-work version of the **waste knot** (see 'Basic Techniques' on page 21) and is a technique that secures your wool.

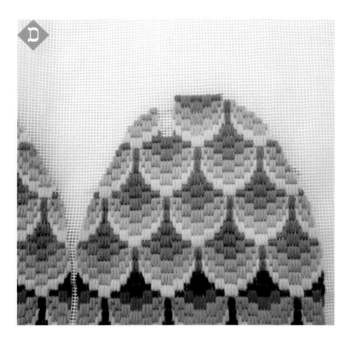

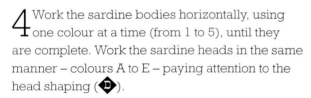

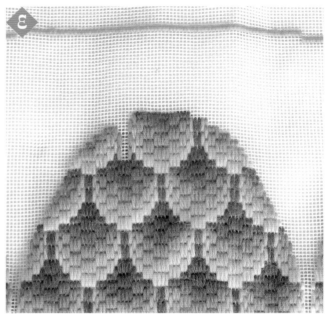

4 Work the sardine bodies horizontally, using one colour at a time (from 1 to 5), until they are complete. Work the sardine heads in the same manner – colours A to E – paying attention to the head shaping ().

TRICK! For this design, you can stitch each vertical stitch from either bottom to top, or top to bottom but this order needs to be adhered to so that the wool at the back of your work is as plentiful as the wool at the front. Where scales are not whole at the bottom edge of the design or around the shaping of the head, stitch over two or four threads of canvas as shown in the chart.

5 Now you can start to work the sardine mouths – in stitches that are four threads of canvas in length – before stitching the outer tin edge in twos, to form a holding line for the cushion's background (❖)

TRICK! You may want to thread five needles, each with a different shade, to have handy – bargello grows quickly and this will save you the time of constantly rethreading the needle.

46

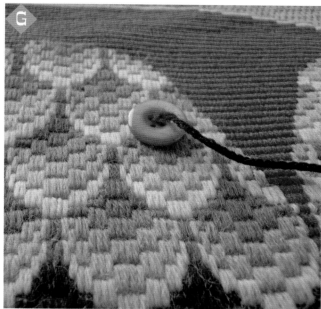

6 Now fill the red tin area with rows of stitches two threads long – this is where you will find you need a fairly thick tapestry wool to prevent the canvas showing through.

7 Work from the bottom right-hand edge to stitch the design background, alternating stitches of two and four in length. This forms a foundation for stitches of four, working as a vertical brick pattern (**F**).

8 Complete the background in this way, working up, then across to the left-hand side of the design and then down, working in twos only when required at the top and bottom edges of the design or where the background meets the sardines.

9 Stitch on the buttons for the sardine eyes, using a dark wool in a cross formation (**G**).

Your design is ready to mount in a frame or make into a cushion, as shown in 'Finishing Techniques' on pages 152–156.

Make it your own!

Once you have completed the Bargello sardine bodies, you can use different stitches for the background, for example, tent or cross stitch (for further information see 'Stitch Glossary' on pages 26–29) for the backgrounds, to create different textures.

Love is in the Air

THIS UPLIFTING WALL HANGING IS SURE TO GET HEARTS RACING,

AND DEMONSTRATES BEAUTIFULLY THE FEELING OF BEING IN LOVE.

USING EDWARDIAN-STYLE figures and a muted colour palette adds an extra romantic note to this circus tale, which will really stand out in a room.

The design is quite straight-forward to make, and is worked in **tent stitch** using the colour chart provided. For further instructions on how to do this, see 'Stitch Glossary' on page 29.

Finished size of design: approx. 26½ x 11in (67 x 28cm).

Equipment

Size 20 tapestry needle

Masking tape

Piece of paper
or straight edge

Pins

Materials

Mono interlock canvas
12 holes per inch
34 x 19in (86 x 48cm) min

Medium-weight cream or pale-coloured cotton backing fabric
Cut to the size of the canvas

Cream thread • 1 spool

Thin black cord, embroidery thread or similar • 1yd (1m)

Heavyweight cotton tape or grosgrain ribbon, 1 ½in (4cm) wide • 40in (1m)

Brass tension rod (or any baton or pole to hang finished piece) • 32in (80cm)

Ribbon/cord, ⅛in (3mm) wide
Approx. 60in (1.5m)

Appleton Bros tapestry wool in the following colours and amounts (available in skeins of 27yd (25m) or hanks of 197yd (180m):

Off White 992 • 110yd (100m)

Bright Terracotta 222
104yd (95m)

Sky Blue 561 • 23yd (21m)

Drab Fawn 951 • 22yd (20m)

Scarlet 504 • 22yd (20m)

Flesh Tints 703 • 10yd (9m)

Dull Rose Pink 148
4½ yd (4m)

Black 993 • 5½ yd (5m)

Flame Red 202 • 13yd (12m)

Dull Marine Blue 323
12yd (11m)

Brown Olive 311 • 5½ yd (5m)

Chocolate 186 • 4½ yd (4m)

Flesh Tints 708 • 2¼ yd (2m)

Mid Blue 153 • 2¼ yd (2m)

Brown Olive 313 • 2¼ yd (2m)

Terracotta 123 • 2¼ yd (2m)

Rose Pink 753 • 1yd (1m)

KEY

- ⌐ Off White 992
- ▦ Bright Terracotta 222
- ⊓ Sky Blue 561
- ⊼ Drab Fawn 951
- ✚ Scarlet 504
- · Flesh Tints 703
- ▤ Dull Rose Pink 148
- ▪ Black 993
- ⊂ Flame Red 202
- ⊠ Dull Marine Blue 323
- ⧄ Brown Olive 311
- ◨ Chocolate 186
- ⌗ Flesh Tints 708
- ⊡ Mid Blue 153
- ⧄ Brown Olive 313
- ⊠ Terracotta 123
- ⧂ Rose Pink 753

Instructions

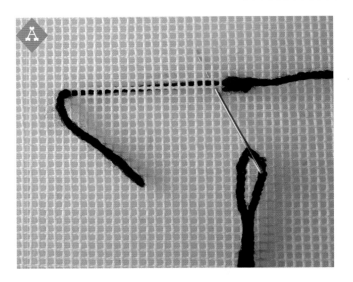

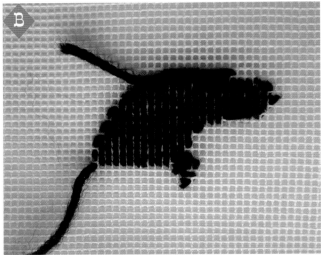

1 Bind the edges of the canvas with masking tape as described in 'Basic Techniques' on page 23, then fold the canvas in half and then in half again. This determines the centre of the design as indicated on the chart. You can either begin at, or near, this centre point, or measure 3in (7.5cm) in from the sides and begin at the edge of the chart.

2 For this design, the male trapeze artist's hair will be stitched first – find the centre of the canvas and then count the squares to the left to find the correct position for his hair.

> **TRICK!** The order of this stitching is only a guide – you can change this order in any way you wish, working some of the background first if you want, or start with the female trapeze artist.

3 Knot one end of the wool, thread the needle and push it front to back about a thumb's length from where you want to begin, opposite where you want to begin stitching. Bring the needle up in your starting place – in this case, the male trapeze artist's hair – and start stitching towards the knot, covering the thread at the back. This is the best method for beginning a colour and you should try to do this method throughout. Once you get near to the knot, carefully snip it off. This is the canvaswork version of the **waste knot** (see 'Basic Techniques' on page 21) (**A**).

4 Once you have finished the male trapeze artists hair (**B**), finish the wool by running your needle through the stitches at the back of your work. Do not run the black wool over the back to begin the eyes and moustache, as this will show through the flesh colour of his face.

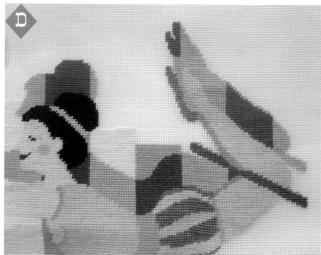

5 Begin to stitch the figures, starting with the male figure, his clothing and trapeze bar (**C**). The waste knot method of beginning a colour is a good method to use throughout the design, as it ensures no 'show through' of one colour under another.

TRICK! When you complete a colour and want to finish it off, always run the wool behind stitches of the same colour to avoid 'show through'. It's best to use lengths of wool around 30in (75cm) long – if your wool is too long, it will become thin and break. If you see this happening, start with a new piece.

6 Stitch the heart and then the female figure before beginning to add the striped shadow to both figures (**D**).

7 Continue stitching the striped background until you have completed the design (**E**). You will need to stretch your work to ensure that it is rectangular and not pulling to one side. This is known as 'blocking' – see 'Finishing Techniques' on page 152 for further information.

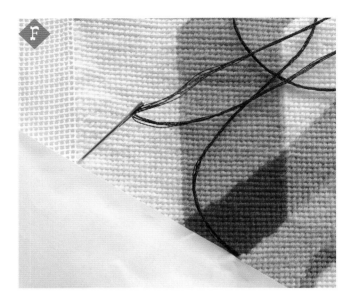

8 Take a length of the black fine cord or embroidery thread and knot it at one end. Using a straight edge such as a piece of paper as a guide, make long stitches from the male trapeze artist's trapeze bar to the edge of the design, putting the needle behind the work where the cord meets the leg. Make sure the thread lies flat and do not pull too tightly or too loosely. Finish the thread by knotting it securely, snip leaving a small 'tail'.

9 Make a parallel line at the other end of the trapeze bar and then repeat this stitching at the opposite side for the female trapeze artist (**F**).

10 Trim the canvas so there is an even surplus around your work. Cut five 8in (20cm) lengths of the cotton tape or ribbon. Fold these lengths in half and place them on the right side of your work and over the hem allowance. The outer two loops are $1/5$in (0.5cm) in from the side edges – the other loops are spaced equally. Secure the loops by pinning (**G**).

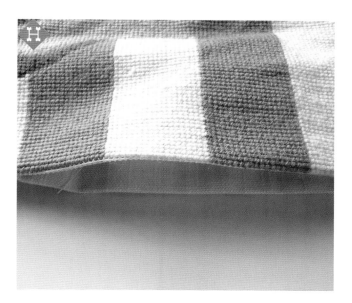

11 Place the backing fabric – this design used cream casement fabric – over your work, right sides together, and pin. With the canvas side up, machine sew or **back stitch** (see 'Stitch Glossary' on page 26) around the canvas, leaving a gap at the bottom edge to turn the work inside out.

12 Trim the corners and seam allowances and turn the design right side out again. Press the backing fabric with an iron (on wool setting), so that the stitched surface is face down. If you want to press the right side of the design, place a clean white cloth over your wall hanging and press through.

13 **Slip stitch** (see 'Stitch Glossary' on page 28) closed the opening at the bottom edge (◆H◆) before inserting a rod through the loops – this design used a brass tension rod, but you can use whatever style you prefer.

14 Now you can tie a ribbon or cord at both ends to create a hanger for the finished design (◆I◆).

Make it your own!

Add 'bling' to this design by stitching any number of flat-backed crystals to the heart – or you could stitch the heart with a mix of wool and metallic thread to catch the light and give added sparkle.

✱✱✱
Fish Tattoo

BASED ON TRADITIONAL TATTOO DESIGNS, THIS QUIRKY LITTLE BAG
IS SURE TO CATCH ADMIRING GLANCES.

THERE'S SOMETHING VERY appealing about accessories worked in needlepoint. The handcrafted detailing involved adds an elegant dimension not found in mass-produced items. This is the sort of bag you want to cherish and keep wrapped in tissue paper when you are not using it.

By following the step-by-step guide, you will find that this bag is easier than it looks to make – enjoy the reaction when you tell people it was all your own work!

This design is worked in counted **cross stitch** from the colour chart provided. For instructions on how to do this, see 'Stitch Glossary' on page 27.

Finished size of design: 8½ x 5in (21 x 12.5cm).

Materials

Double tapestry canvas, 12 holes per inch
You will need the width of your finished bag plus at least 6in (20cm) and double the depth of your bag plus at least 6in (20cm) or 12in (40cm) if you are using a frame.

Appleton Bros crewel wool in the following colours and amounts (available in skeins of 27yd (25m) or hanks of 197yd (180m):

Dull Marine Blue 328
61yd (55m)

White 991 • 29yd (26m)

Bright China Blue 745
22yd (20m)

Flamingo 625 • 44yd (40m)

Coral 861 • 22yd (20m)

Kingfisher 481 • 28yd (25m)

Bright Yellow 552 • 18yd (16m)

Cherry Red 995 • 11yd (10m)

Sea Green 403 • 3yd (2m)

Turquoise 521 • 219yd (200m)

Lining fabric
8½ x 5in (21 x 12.5cm) plus seam allowance

Machine thread to match design background colour
1 spool

Brown parcel paper

Seed pearl beads
As many as you like

Strong fabric glue

Equipment

Size 22 tapestry needle

Marker pen

Masking tape

Beading needle

9in (23cm) metal purse frame

Wooden needlepoint/ tapestry frame (optional), **to accommodate width of canvas**

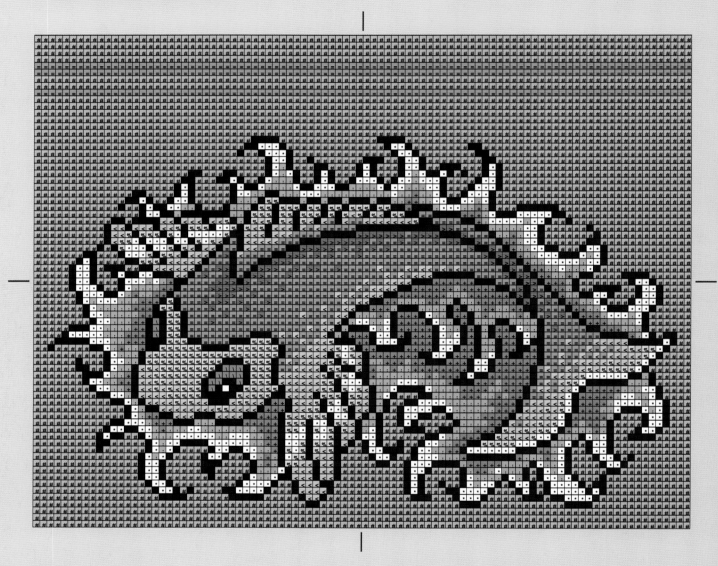

KEY

■ Dull Marine Blue 328	✚ Bright China Blue 745	◿ Coral 861	⊘ Bright Yellow 552	⍀ Sea Green 403
★ White 991	⊟ Flamingo 625	⠒ Kingfisher 481	▷ Cherry Red 995	# Turquoise 521

Instructions

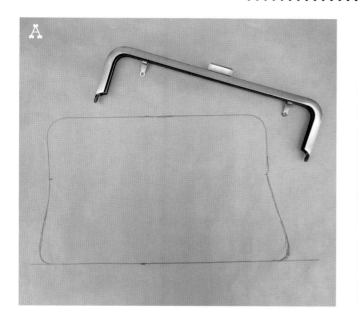

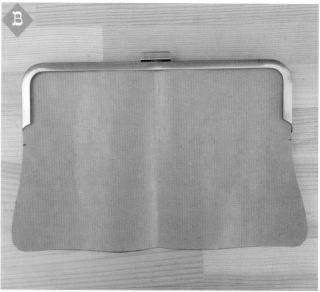

1 Bind the edges of the canvas with masking tape as described in 'Basic Techniques' on page 23 and place the bag handles on a large sheet of paper.

2 Draw around the handle with a marker pen, marking the hinge. Draw the shape you want your finished bag to be (it could be a square-shaped bag or one that flares at the bottom, for example), keeping in mind the size of the design area, as the design will need to fit on comfortably with the background colour all round (Ⓐ).

3 Cut this shape out of the paper, then fold it in half and trim to ensure the design is symmetrical.

4 Place your paper pattern inside the handles and adjust the fit if necessary by trimming the excess. The paper pattern should lie flat inside the handles, just touching all inside edges (Ⓑ).

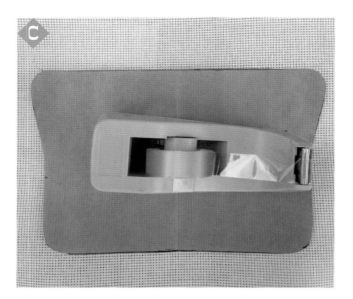

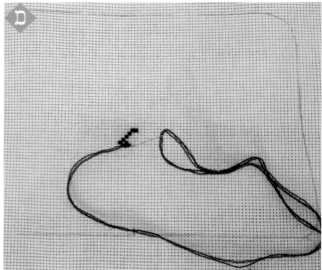

5 Lay the paper pattern onto the canvas, weighing it down and ensuring that the centre fold lines up with the weave of the canvas before drawing around the pattern, marking the middle fold.

6 Flip the pattern over, weigh it down again and draw around it so that the bag is symmetrical (), then fold the paper pattern in half and in half again to get your centre point. Now place the pattern onto the canvas and mark it on both halves of the bag.

> **TRICK!** If you are using a frame, attach the canvas to the frame with a **slip stitch** (see 'Stitch Glossary' on page 28). This keeps a perfect shape to the work and the canvas will not need to be stretched afterwards.

7 Stitch the outline of the fish and waves, starting from the centre, as marked on the chart. Fold the wool in half and thread it through the needle, leaving the looped end longer than the cut end. Secure the first stitch by pulling the wool through the canvas from the back to the front, leaving the looped end hanging, then stitching the first diagonal of the cross stitch (D).

> **TRICK!** You may find it easier to mark the centre of each stitch with a permanent marker.

8 With the outline completed on both halves of the bag (**E**), you can stitch the colours within the outline, beginning with the blue tones in the waves (**F**) before stitching in the body of the fish.

9 Now fill in the grey background colour up to the drawn line, as well as the two orange stripes that should rest just below the bag frame (**G**).

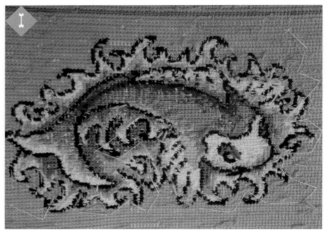

10 Add the 'whiskers' on the fish, as shown in the detail chart, using **back stitch** (see 'Stitch Glossary' on page 26) with two strands of Dull Marine Blue 328 ().

11 Before you bead the bag, place the small seed pearls randomly around the fish and in the waves, to see what amount works best. Do not bead too close to the edges, as these will need to be kept clear for the construction of the bag. Now attach the beads using two strands of cotton thread. Stitch each bead in place and stitch again to secure (❖).

12 Trim the canvas and fold it in half along the centre point (❖). Mark on the wrong side of your work where the hinge of the frame will rest and stitch the edges of the bag up to this point.

13 Trim the corners of the canvas and turn the bag inside out. Using your original pattern piece, place the bottom edge of the pattern on to the fold of your lining material and draw around it.

14 Cut out the shape, being sure to add enough fabric for a seam (**K**). Machine sew or back stitch as with the bag, leaving the sides open above the hinge area.

15 Without turning the lining the right side out, place it inside the bag. Open out the seams on both the bag and the lining. Clip the corners and turn in the seam allowance on the bag and the lining (**L**).

16 Slip stitch the lining to the bag (**M**). This does not have to be overly neat, as it will be hidden inside the bag frame. Glue the frame to the bag, following the manufacturer's instructions.

Make it your own!

For a brighter bag, choose bolder wool colours. Handles are also available in many shapes and finishes, plus you could add glass beads for a 'bubble effect'.

Passion

LIVING A PASSIONATE LIFE IS MOST DEFINITELY THE WAY FORWARD... FOLLOW YOUR HEART AND EXPRESS 'THE FIRE INSIDE' WITH THIS EXCITING CUSHION.

INSPIRED BY CLASSIC HEART tattoos and rock couture, this piece has a chic designer feel thanks to its striking lettering and strong colours. The grey background compliments and enhances the heat of the flames for an eye-catching look.

This design is worked in counted **cross stitch** from the colour chart provided. To see how to do this, see the 'Stitch Glossary' on page 27, and be sure to pay particular attention to the shading in the colour chart, in order to get the detail just right.

Finished size of design: approx. 16 x 15½in (40.5 x 39cm).

Materials

Mono interlock canvas
10 holes per inch
22in (56cm) square minimum

Appleton Bros crewel wool
in the following amounts
(available in skeins of
27yd (25m) or hanks
of 197yd (180m):

Iron Grey 963 • 383yd (350m)

White 991 • 28yd (25m)

Bright Mauve 455
110yd (100m)

Dull Gold 855 • 39yd (35m)

Black 993 • 39yd (35m)

Scarlet 505 • 36yd (33m)

Scarlet 504 • 36yd (33m)

Orange Red 447 • 24yd (22m)

Scarlet 501A • 25yd (23m)

Bright Yellow 552 • 31yd (28m)

Bright Yellow 555 • 27yd (24m)

Orange Red 443 • 22yd (20m)

Flat-backed fire opal crystals
¼in (5mm) wide
Approx. 25

Equipment

Size 20 tapestry needle

Masking tape

Matching clamps

Clamping tool

Wooden tapestry frame
(optional)

KEY

⊡ Iron Grey 963	⊘ Dull Gold 855	② Scarlet 504	⏊ Bright Yellow 552
☐ White 991	■ Black 993	③ Orange Red 447	∼ Bright Yellow 555
⊞ Bright Mauve 455	⊣ Scarlet 505	④ Scarlet 501A	▲ Orange Red 443

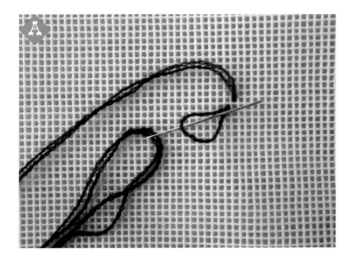

1 Bind the edges of the canvas with masking tape as described in 'Basic Techniques' on page 23. A frame is not needed, but if you prefer to use one, pick one that accommodates the cut canvas easily, with at least 2in (5cm) either side of the cut edge. Fold the canvas in half and then in half again – this determines the centre of the design as indicated on the chart. You can either begin at, or near, this centre point, or measure 3in (7.5cm) in from the sides and begin at the edge of the chart.

2 Begin by working the drop shadow of the letters in black, with those nearest to your starting place. Fold the wool in half and thread it through the needle, leaving the looped end longer than the cut end. Secure the first stitch by pulling the wool through the canvas from the back to the front, leaving the looped end hanging, then stitching the first diagonal of the cross stitch (A).

3 Once you've completed the black shadow of the lettering (B), including the line running underneath the letters, work the outer white line of the flames, starting near the 'P' or the 'N' (C).

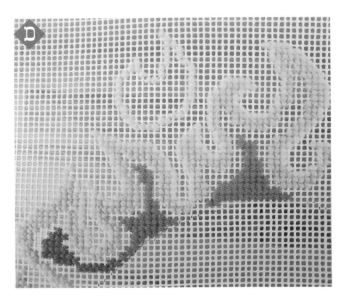

4 Begin filling in the orange and yellow colours of the flames, starting with the yellow (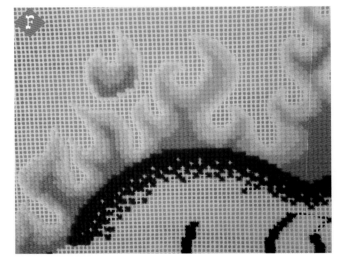D) and not forgetting the section beneath the letters (E).

5 Start on the heart itself, first stitching the darkest red area around its outer edge. Pay special attention to the key here, to ensure that the two red colours will blend properly (F).

> **TRICK!** If you are using a frame, attach the canvas to the frame with a **slip stitch** (see 'Stitch Glossary' on page 28). This keeps a perfect shape to the work and the canvas will not need to be stretched afterwards.

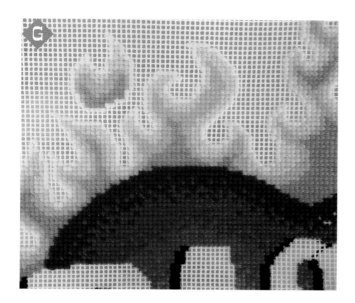

6 Now fill the lighter red area of the heart, up to the edge of the lettering and any areas of black drop shadow (**G**).

> **TRICK!** When you have shaded areas in, such as the heart, you will find it easier to stitch alternate bands of colour. For example, once you have stitched the darkest red, you could miss the next tone and go for the third band of red. This way, you can fill in with the remaining shades without referring so closely to the chart.

7 Work the purple interior of the letters (**H**) and their gold shadow. You can either do one letter at a time or do the shadow and then the filling for all the letters. Remember to include the line running underneath the letters (**I**).

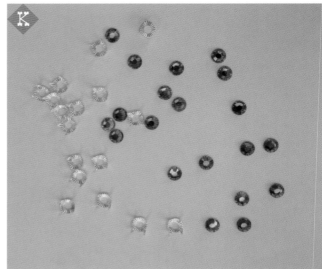

8 Stitch the grey background around the design and right up to the design edges ( J). This completes the chart and now you are ready to add some sparkle.

TRICK! These steps are presented in a logical progression, filling in the background after the design elements have been worked. You may prefer to work some of the background as you go, so that it does not feel too monotonous at the end!

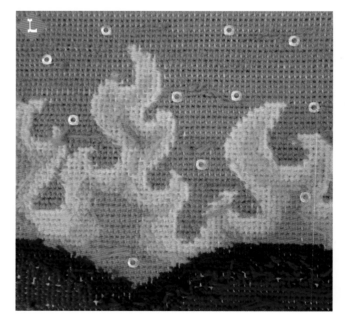

9 Select the number of fire opal crystals you wish to use (this design uses 24) with their matching backs (K).

10 Lay the crystals on the design first before you secure them, to give you an idea of the finished effect (L).

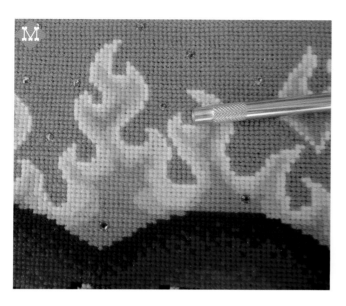

11 Push the clamps through the back of the work, letting them find a natural gap in the work – do not force them, as they may cut through the canvas.

12 Turn your work right side up and place the crystal in the four points of the clamp. Using the clamping tool, push down to secure (◆M◆).

13 Continue to add as many crystals as you like, for the finished design (◆N◆).

Your design is ready to stretch and frame or make into a cushion as shown in 'Finishing Techniques' on pages 152–156.

Make it your own!

The fire opal crystals are often bought in packs of 35, so you can add or subtract the amount to suit your taste.

CHAPTER 2

Appliqué

APPLIQUÉ

THE ART OF APPLIQUÉ IS SIMPLY APPLYING FABRIC TO FABRIC, AND WITH SO MANY STUNNING MODERN AND VINTAGE TEXTILES AVAILABLE TODAY, WHAT BETTER TIME TO HAVE A GO?

APPLIQUÉ IS ONE of the fastest forms of embroidery and once you know the basics you can really let your imagination run wild. Applied fabric has and is still used to create large banners, as it is less costly to produce than solid embroidery. It is also used widely in quilting. The word 'appliqué' is derived from the French 'appliquer', which means 'to put on or lay on'. It is believed to have originated from being a way of patching holes and using up scraps of fabrics but it quickly evolved into a needlework technique in its own right.

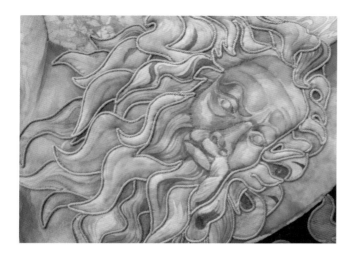

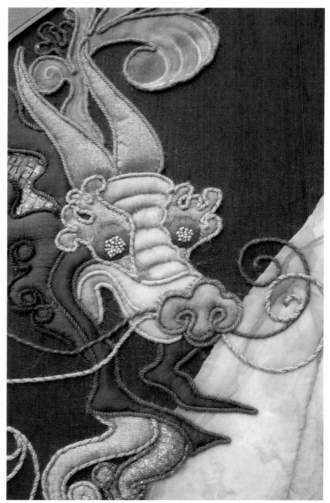

Many different cultures use appliqué – in India it can be found in a variety of types of folk art, often depicting plants, animals and mythical characters. In Africa, applied fabrics have been used to document historic events. Native Americans based their designs on traditional body paint and created pieces that could then be turned into pillow cases, quilts and placemats. Throughout the world, appliqué has been used to document history and culture.

THE PROJECTS

Appliqué can also be used as a base for embroidery and other types of embellishment and is perfect for decorating clothes and creating cushions and hangings. It lends itself beautifully to three-dimensional work, as layers of padding and fabric can be built up gradually. In this chapter you have three projects to choose from, each with a very different vibe. Adorn your shoulders with our *Bleeding Rose*, skip towards Victoriana and make our *Rabbit in a Top Hat* picture or go wild for our *One* cushion!

Opposite: Detail of Pheonix by **Jenny Adin Christie**; *Top left: Detail of Atlas by* **Jenny Adin Christie**; *Middle: Appliqué cushions by* **Kate Farrer**; *Top right: Appliqué by* **Nicola Jarvis**; *Bottom right: Detail of Dragon by* **Jenny Adin Christie**

Rabbit in a Top Hat

HERE IS A PLAY ON THE POPULAR CLASSIC SILHOUETTE FORM.
THE RABBIT HAS A CERTAIN QUIRKY VICTORIAN CHARM
IN HIS TOP HAT AND BOW TIE.

RABBITS ARE KNOWN as a symbol of good luck, and bring back memories of the famous Peter, Br'er and Roger Rabbits. And who can forget, of course, the Easter bunny?

The use of different fabrics, ribbons and cords adds texture and elegance to the piece while the padding gives it dimension. You can follow the instructions here to create our bunny or use it as an inspiration piece to design your own silhouette.

Finished size of design: $8\frac{1}{2}$ x $5\frac{1}{2}$in (21.8 x 14cm).

Materials

Calico
18 x 16in (45 x 40cm)

Pink and green velvet ribbons
80in (2m) of each

Pink felt
16in (40cm) square

Pink stripe cotton
10in (25cm) square

Black faux suede
10in (25cm) square

Machine thread to match fabric
1 reel of each colour

Black cord
16in (40cm)

Black stranded cotton
1 skein

Equipment

12in (30cm) clip frame

Needles

Sharp pair of scissors

Paper scissors

Pencil

White-coloured pencil

Pins

Stiletto (optional)

Quilter's pencil (optional)

Light box (optional)

NB The calico as well as the pink and green velvet ribbons need to fit a 12in (30cm) clip frame.

78

Instructions

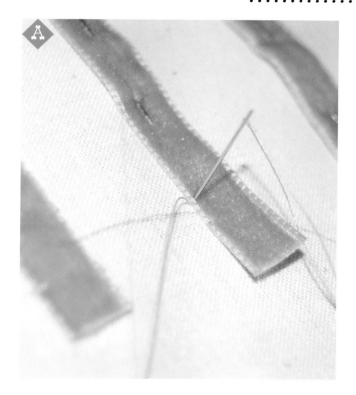

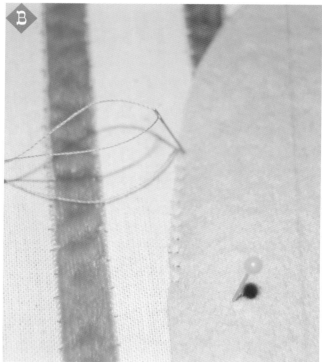

1 Photocopy the design a few times so you have extra copies to cut up and make notes on as you work through the project. Trace the outline of the oval shape on to your calico, which will act as your base fabric. A quilter's pencil is very useful for this, as the lines don't smudge.

2 Put your work into your frame and pull tight. Lay on the velvet ribbons around the oval with approximately ½in (2cm) gap between each. Pin in place and cut away any excess from the middle of the oval. **Stab stitch** (see 'Stitch Glossary' on page 28) the ribbons down using machine thread (Ⓐ).

3 Cut the oval shape out of one of your paper copies, lay it on to the pink felt and draw round it twice. Cut the shapes out of the felt, and then trim one down so it fits inside the oval with approximately ⅛in (3mm) gap around the outside. First stab stitch the smaller oval on, and then stitch the larger one on top (Ⓑ).

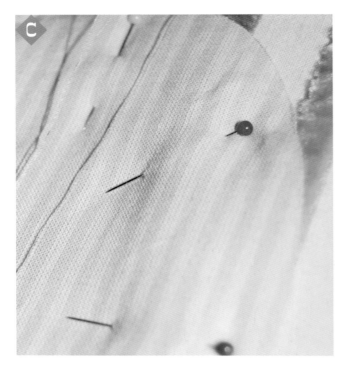

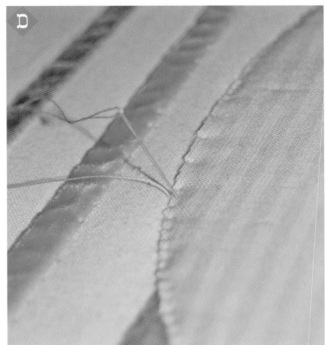

4 Trace the oval shape on to the striped cotton and cut out. Pin the oval in place (C) and stab stitch around the outside (D).

5 Cut the rabbit out of the paper, place on to the black suede and draw around it with a white-coloured pencil. Cut the rabbit out and pin it in place in the centre of the oval. Stab stitch in place (E).

6 **Couch** (see 'Stitch Glossary' on page 26) six strands of black cotton, using one strand of black cotton around the edge to cover your stab stitch. Lay the threads down around the edge of the rabbit and stitch over the top of them; your stitches should again be around ⅛in (3mm) apart (◆F◆).

TRICK! In order for your couched threads to lay down neatly, separate all of the strands and then put them together again before couching.

7 Once you've stitched around the shape, you'll need to plunge the ends of the couched thread. Make a hole in the fabric where you want to plunge them, using a stiletto or a large needle. Then cut a piece of thread around 8in (20cm) long, fold in half and put one end through the eye of your needle. You now should have a loop coming from one side of the eye and the two ends coming from the other.

TRICK! Plunge your ends on the point of the shape rather than on a straight edge or a curve. This creates a good point and keeps the couching from looking disjointed.

8 Put the needle through the hole, catch the ends of your couched threads with the loop and pull them through to the back (◆G◆). Then turn your frame over and stitch down these loose ends on the back.

9 Next, stitch black lines on for the whiskers. **Stem stitch** (see 'Stitch Glossary' on page 29) is used here, but you can use any outline stitch you choose (◆H).

10 You then need to stitch the cord on to cover the raw edge and stitches on the oval, to make a kind of frame. Lay the cord down and stitch into it, leaving approximately ⅓in (1cm) between each stitch (◆I).

11 Make a hole in the fabric using a stiletto or large needle, plunge the ends of the cord through, stitch down and secure the cord on the back as with the stranded cotton to complete the design (◆J).

Make it your own!

Why not do a silhouette of a family member, friend or even yourself? Simply take a photograph of the person in profile and trace the outline. Animals make great silhouettes, or why not embellish the rabbit with beads and small found objects to evoke the magic of *Alice in Wonderland*.

The design is ready to stretch and frame, shown in 'Finishing Techniques' on pages 152–154.

82

✳ ✳ ✳

Bleeding Rose

A BEAUTIFUL RED ROSE IS OFTEN THE SYMBOL OF LOVE, AN EMOTION THAT CAN FILL US WITH JOY AND PAIN IN EQUAL MEASURE. CAPTURE THESE CONTRADICTORY FEELINGS WITH THIS APPLIQUÉ OF A PERFECT, BLEEDING ROSE.

THIS DESIGN IS MADE up of simple repeating elements. Triangles of silk form the rose shape with turned edges for a clean, neat finish.

Stitch your rose in an endless choice of coloured silks or use other types of fabric to create different textures – or you can embellish it with beads, stones, crystals and free embroidery, to whatever suits your style. This design will look fantastic on all kinds of clothing, new or old: shirts, blazers, skirts – even on a special black dress.

Finished size: 5⅝ x 4⅝in (14.4 x 11.7cm).

Materials

Item of clothing

Orange silk
12in (30cm) square

Iron-on transfer adhesive
20in (50cm)

Orange machine thread
(to match fabric)
1 reel

Pink drop beads
As many as you like

Red metallic thread
1 skein or reel

Equipment

8in (20cm) ring frame

Sharp pair of scissors

Needles

Curved needle

Small screwdriver

Paper scissors

White colouring pencil

Pencil

Pins

Mini iron (optional)

Stiletto (optional)

Instructions

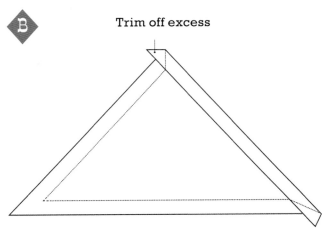

Trim off excess

1 Photocopy the design from the book a few times so you have extra copies to cut up and make notes on as you go through the project. Cut the shapes out of the paper, creating a stencil. Put your fabric or item of clothing into your ring frame, pulling it as tight as possible, and lay the stencil on the top (**A**). Trace the design outline using a white pencil and a ruler in order to get straight lines.

TRICK! Once you've transferred the design, try on the piece of clothing to check the positioning. If you're not happy, just wash it and start again.

2 Using the paper shapes that you cut out to make the stencil, turn them over, place them on to the paper side of the iron-on adhesive and draw around them using a pencil (you might like to number the triangles so that you don't lose track of which one's which). Do this rather than drawing around the stencil to transfer the design on to the adhesive, otherwise the edges of the shapes won't cover the design lines. Cut them out and iron them on to the silk,

on medium heat. Now cut around the ironed-on silk shapes, leaving an excess of about ¼in (5mm) of fabric around the edges.

3 One by one, remove the iron-on adhesive's paper from the back of the silk shape and fold over each edge of the triangle, ironing them in place as you go, to get a 'hemmed edge'.

TRICK! Buy iron-on transfer adhesive by the metre, as packets sometimes have narrow pieces. Allow the adhesive to cool before removing the paper. This ensures that the glue holds to the fabric, rather than peeling off with the paper.

4 After ironing each triangle's edge back on itself, cut away any excess fabric from the corner before turning over the joining edge (**B**). Don't worry too much if the corners aren't perfect at this stage – you can manipulate them into place when you come to stitch them down.

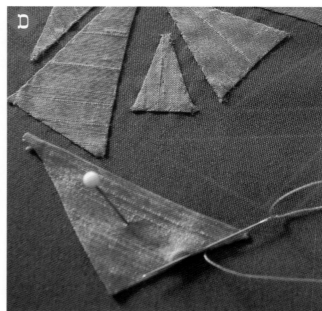

5 Now you can begin to stich the 'hemmed' triangles on to your item of clothing. Start your thread off in the corner of shape number 1 (if you have numbered your triangles), using the **waste knot** technique (see 'Basic Techniques' on page 21) to secure the thread. Place the first shape on to the outlined design and hold it in place with a pin.

6 Begin by stitching down the corner, coming up on the outside of the shape and going down into it (**C**). Do three **stab stitches** (See 'Stitch Glossary' on page 28) on the corner before continuing down the edge, **slip stitching** (See 'Stitch Glossary' on page 28) it as you go (**D**). At this point you can use a curved needle if you find that easier (**E**). When you reach the next corner, again do three stab stitches to hold it in place. Continue in this way until all the shapes have been stitched down.

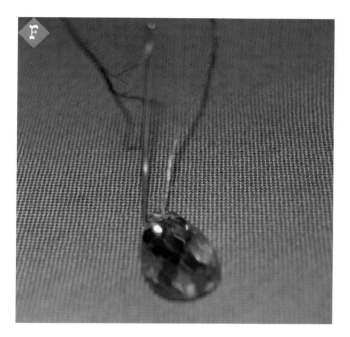

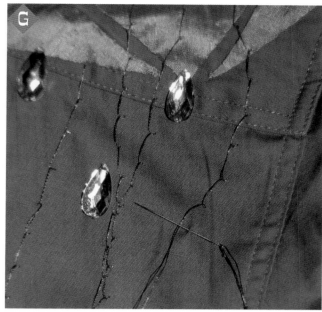

7 If you wish to add beads you can do so at this
stage. This design uses drop beads, which
have holes at the top and bottom, but you could use
whatever stones or beads you like. If using drop
beads, simply do a few stitches through the holes
with the amount of beads to suit your taste (**F**).

8 Now you can do some decorative stitching to
give the impression of blood. This design uses
a **buttonhole stitch** (See 'Stitch Glossary' on page
26), with long stitches that are intentionally loose to
give a flowing yet disjointed finish to the completed
piece (**G**).

Make it your own!

Be playful with colour and size, using whichever
decorative stitches you know and like. You can
even add more beads and stones for extra bling!

One

THIS PICTURE SAYS IT ALL WITHOUT RESORTING TO POETRY – WHEN WE TRULY LOVE, THE BOUNDARIES OF OUR SEPARATE LIVES MELT AWAY AND TWO BECOME ONE.

THE COLOURS OF LOVE don't have to be soft and sentimental, and this design can be as outrageous as you wish. Throw pink against green, emblazon with diamante and stitch together with golden thread.

Using a clever combination of appliqué, reverse appliqué and padding to give dimension, this project also utilizes a variety of fabrics, threads and stones to add texture.

The finished piece makes a wonderful gift to celebrate any union.

Finished size of design: 8in (20.5cm) square.

Materials

White calico (bleached)
15in (38cm) square

Red, purple and white felt
10in (25cm) square

Pink and green silk
15in (38cm) square

Purple cotton and red silk
10in (25cm) square

Iron-on transfer adhesive
20in (50cm) square

**Machine thread
to match your fabric**
1 reel of each colour

**Red, purple and pink
stranded cotton, to match
your fabric**
1 skein of each colour

Silver Japanese thread
20in (50cm) piece

Tracing paper

Swarovski crystals and beads
(optional)

Equipment

10in (25cm) ring frame

Sharp pair of scissors

Needles

Small screwdriver

Paper scissors

Pencil

Pins

Mini iron (optional)

Stiletto (optional)

Light box (optional)

Quilter's pencil (optional)

Instructions

· ·

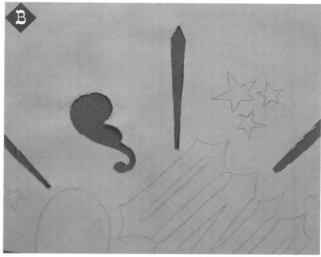

1 Photocopy the design a few times so you have extra copies to cut up and make notes on as you go through the project. Cut the white calico, and pink and green silks to fit a 10in (25cm) ring frame.

2 Transfer the design on to the green silk. You can do this using a light box or by taping the design on to a window, and taping the fabric over the top. The light coming from behind should make it possible to see the design through it. This allows you to trace the design on to your silk – a quilter's pencil is useful for this, as the lines don't smudge (◆A◆).

3 You now need to cut three squares of the iron-on adhesive, the same size as your cut out fabrics. Iron one piece on to the calico, remove the paper and iron the pink silk on the top. Iron the other piece of adhesive on to the back of the green silk. Before removing the paper, cut out the scrolls and the rays using a sharp pair of small scissors. Once you have cut them all out, remove the paper and iron the green silk on top of the pink silk, on a medium setting. The pink should now be showing through from the back (◆B◆). This technique is called reverse appliqué.

TRICK! Buy iron-on transfer adhesive by the metre, as packets sometimes have narrow pieces. Allow the adhesive to cool before removing the paper. This ensures that the glue holds to the fabric, rather than peeling off with the paper.

4 Put your work in to your ring frame and pull the fabric as tight as possible. Use a small screwdriver to tighten up the frame.

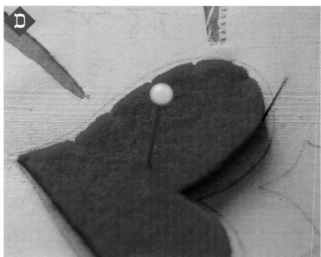

5 Using the green machine thread, **stab stitch** (see 'Stitch Glossary' on page 28) around each of the rays and scrolls, bringing your needle up through the pink fabric and taking it down through the green (). Keep your stitches quite small so they don't show underneath the edging, which you'll do later on. Your stitches should be about ⅛in (3mm) apart. Although you are going to cover up these stitches later on, it's important to do this so that all of the layers are securely fixed together.

TRICK! Use as small a needle as you can – this makes sewing through the layers easier.

6 Next, cut the hearts and the letters out of one of your paper copies of the design. Place the hearts on to the red felt, pin in place and cut out. You'll need to cut out two pieces of felt for each heart. Trim one of each heart down so it fits inside the design. Now pin the letters on the purple felt and cut them out, only needing one of each letter.

7 Starting with one of the smaller hearts, place it onto the green fabric and put a pin through the middle to hold in place. Stab stitch around the edge, but this time leave gaps of about ⅓in (1cm) in between your stitches to hold the felt in place (). Stab stitch around the felt again, filling in the gaps between your stitches. Now place the second layer over the top and stab stitch this one in place. Repeat this process with the other heart and the letters, although for the letters you only need one layer of felt.

8 Now trace just the letters and the hearts off the photocopied design. Turn the tracing over, place a piece of adhesive over the top, paper side up, and trace the letters and the hearts on to the adhesive. Iron the hearts on to the red silk and the letters on to the purple cotton. Cut the hearts and the letters out and remove the paper.

9 One by one, iron the hearts and letters onto your project and stab stitch around the outside. Do them one by one – if you iron them all on and then do the stitching this may result in the fabrics fraying. A mini iron can be very useful for ironing on these small pieces, although you can also use a standard iron.

10 Now you have applied all of the fabrics, it's time to do the decorative stitching around the edges of everything, apart from the stars. **Couching stitches** (see 'Stitch Glossary' on page 26) have been used throughout, but you can use different stitches if you wish. The couching is done using stranded cotton – in this case, six strands for the letters and eight strands for the hearts and rays. These are couched down with one strand of the cotton.

TRICK! In order for your couched threads to lay down neatly, separate all of the strands and then put them together again before couching.

11 Lay the threads down – each set of threads should match the colour of the shape you're stitching around – and stitch over the top of them. Your stitches should again be around ⅛in (3mm) apart (◆E).

12 Once you've stitched round one of the shapes, you'll need to plunge the ends of the couched thread. Make a hole in the fabric where you want to plunge them, using a stiletto or a large needle. Cut a piece of thread around 8in (20cm) long, fold it in half and put one end through the eye of your needle. You now should have a loop coming from one side of the eye and the two ends coming for the other. Put the needle through the hole, catch the ends of your couched threads with the loop and pull them through to the back (◆F).

TRICK! Plunge your ends on the point of the shape rather than on a straight edge or a curve. This creates a good point and avoids the couching from looking disjointed.

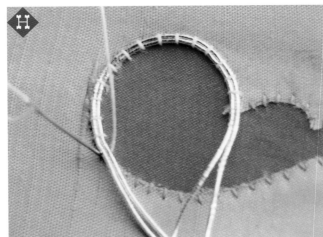

13 Once you've done all your couched stitching around the edges of the shapes, turn your frame over and stitch down these loose ends on the back (◆G).

14 Repeat the same process of stitching around the edges of the shapes, this time with the Japanese thread on the scrolls only, couching down two strands of it together (◆H).

15 Finally, cut out the stars in paper, place them on to the white felt and cut them out before simply stab stitching them in place (◆I).

16 Now that the stitching is finished you can add any number of Swarovski crystals or any other type of beads or stones (◆J).

Your design is ready to frame or put on a cushion, as shown in 'Finishing Techniques' on pages 152–156.

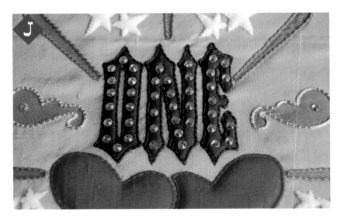

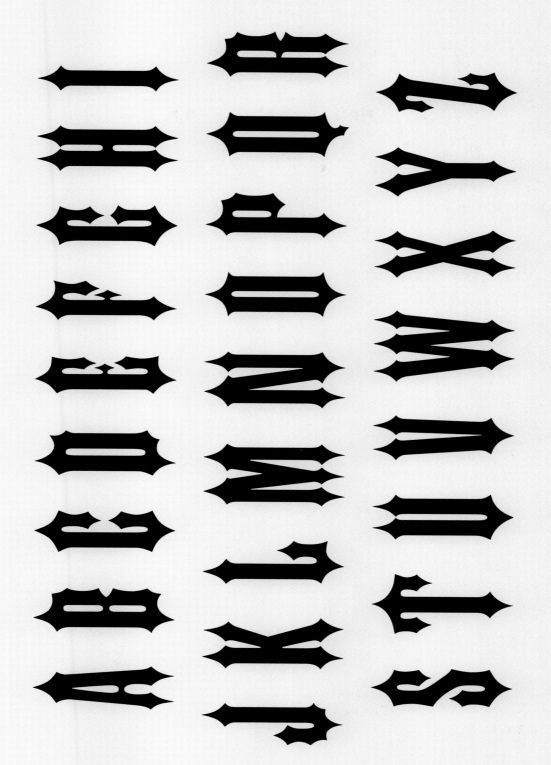

97

Silk Shading

3

SILK SHADING

SILK SHADING LENDS ITSELF BEAUTIFULLY TO DEPICTIONS OF PLANTS,
FLOWERS AND ANIMALS, THE IDEA BEING TO MAKE THE IMAGE AS TRUE
TO LIFE AS POSSIBLE.

ALSO KNOWN AS PAINTING with a needle, silk shading was believed to be first used in China over 5,000 years ago; how it came to be used in other countries is unknown. Historically, the technique has been used alongside goldwork in ecclesiastical work and was also used on court dress. In Victorian times, silk shading lost its appeal during the fashion for Berlin woolwork, but interest was soon revived and the technique was used widely throughout the Arts and Crafts Movement in the late 1800s and early 1900s.

Today, silk shading is seen as a technique that only the most accomplished embroiderers can produce – this is simply not true! Keep in mind that it is painting with a needle, a free and creative form of embroidery with few rules. Having said that, you don't have to be brilliant at painting to be able to work this technique, as a needle and thread are very different tools to paints and a brush.

The stitch used is called 'long and short' – however this name is very misleading. The term 'long and short' suggests that the sizes of your stitches should be regimented and this is not the case. The more random your stitching, the more blended the colours will be. This technique is very forgiving – you don't want to overwork any areas but where the colours aren't as blended as you would like, you can slip in extra stitches here and there. Nowadays it is quite common for silk shading to be worked in stranded cottons, as they are easier to work with than silk, are a little thicker and perish more slowly.

THE PROJECTS

If you are new to silk shading, start with the *Golden Apple*, the first project in this chapter. This is a simple shape and will give you the opportunity to get into the rhythm of stitching and blending. The *Kissing Couple* curtains throw all the rules out of the window, leaving open spaces and suggestions of shading; if you prefer a more organic approach that uses stitch as a mark-making technique, go for this project. Last, but certainly not least, is the beautiful *Bird in Flight*. This project is worked in silk threads, which lend a luxurious feel to stunning effect. With all of the projects, take a relaxed attitude, find your own style and remember that no two people's silk shading will appear the same.

Opposite: Silk shading c/o **Royal School of Needlwork Collection**
Top: Peregrine Falcon by **Lisa Bilby**
Above: Close up of Lady by **Lucy Barter**

Golden Apple

THE APPLE, THE ORIGINAL 'FORBIDDEN FRUIT', IS HISTORICALLY
A SYMBOL OF LOVE AND SEXUALITY, TEMPTATION AND EVIL.
BUT WHAT DOES THIS APPLE MEAN TO YOU? AND WHO IS HOLDING IT?

PERHAPS THIS HAND is the hand of peace, extending friendship – or the evil queen offering it up to Snow White... Or maybe it makes you think of a fresh new start? Or is it simply a beautiful lady holding a golden apple?

This framed picture is perfect if you are new to silk shading. Layers of colour are built up gradually and subtly and the simple elegance of the running stitch shows off the fruit's delicate shading.

Finished size of design: 6¼ x 4¼in (16 x 11cm).

Materials

Natural cotton calico
15in (38cm) square

Anchor stranded cotton
1 skein of each of the
following colours:

278, 281, 300, 306, 400

Equipment

10in (25cm) ring frame

Sharp pair of scissors

Small needles (size 12 or as small as you can manage)

Small screwdriver

Quilter's pencil (optional)

Light box (optional)

104

Instructions

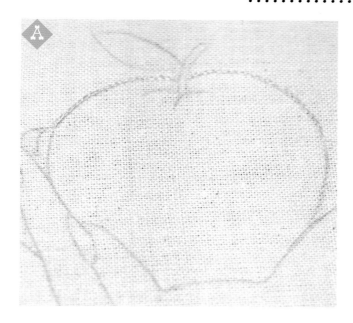

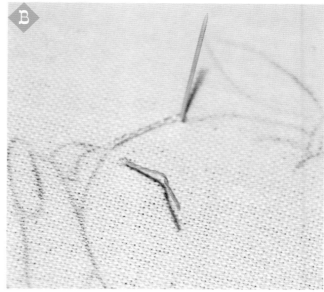

1 Photocopy the design a few times so you have extra copies to make notes on as you go along. You may also find it useful to do a shaded copy in pencil, as this helps to get in your mind where the light and dark areas are.

2 If you have any difficulty seeing the design through the fabric, use a light box (if you have one) or tape the design on to the window and the fabric over the top. Use a quilter's pencil to draw on the design so that the lines don't smudge. This is especially important with silk shading as normal pencils can easily rub off and make your threads dirty. Put the fabric in the ring frame and pull it as tight as you can, tightening up the screw with a small screwdriver as you go.

3 Start with the section that is furthest away from the eye – in this case, the main body of the apple, first doing a **split stitch** (see 'Stitch Glossary' on page 28) edge in one strand of stranded cotton. Your stitches should be no more than $\frac{1}{16}$in (1.5mm) long – they need to be small and secure so that when you work over them the line doesn't shift. The split stitch is covered up by your silk shading but creates a clean neat edge – you won't see it when the project is finished but it really is worth taking the time to do. Only split stitch on an outside edge or next to an area that has already been worked – in this case, it is the two top outside edges of the apple, as the rest is surrounded by the hand. Always do the split stitch in one of the main colours you are going to shade with, to avoid the stitches showing through when you come to stitch over (◆A). It is also important to split stitch just on the outside edge of your design line to avoid it showing (◆B).

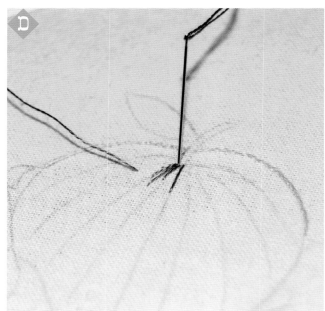

4 The apple is done in natural shading, where the stitches follow the roundness of the shape. In order to get your stitch direction correct you can, if you wish, draw on some direction lines using a quilter's pencil (**C**).

5 The area around the stem is the darkest, so start off with the dark green colour no. 281. Always begin with a stitch in the centre of your shape, bringing your needle up in the shape and down over the outside edge, then continue working outwards from this stitch (**D**). Your smallest stitches should be no smaller than $\frac{1}{8}$in (4mm) and no larger than $\frac{3}{8}$in (1cm). It may feel at first like your stitches are unnaturally long but don't worry about that – when you come to do your second row you will be coming up in the stitches of this first row and will therefore lose some of the length (**E**).

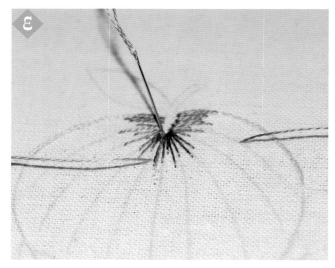

TRICK! Remember, the more variable the lengths of your stitches are, the more blended the piece will appear.

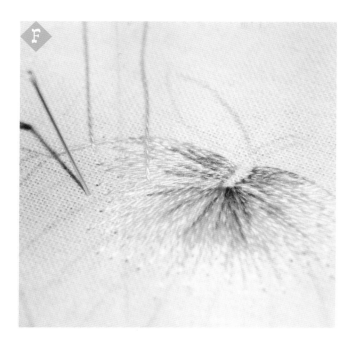

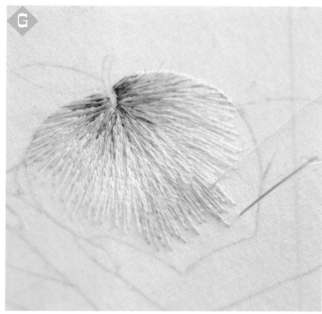

6 Once you have completed your first row, start again in the centre and this time bring your needle up in the stitch of your previous row and take it down in to the shape. Again, continue with the dark green and golden colours. Use the full length of the stitches of the first row, bringing some of your stitches up really quite close to the edge and others much further down. Don't be afraid to be as random as possible – this isn't a regimented form of embroidery so don't try and make it perfect.

TRICK! **When working along the row in one colour, leave gaps in between your stitches to get the stitch direction correct, but also so you can go back and fill in with another colour.**

7 When you come to your third row, start introducing the light green and light yellow colours (**F**).

TRICK! **If you have a thread of one colour on the go and want to use a different colour, you don't have to finish off your thread. Simply bring it up away from the area you're stitching and leave it hanging there until you need it again. Try to always do this within the design though, just in case the coloured thread marks the fabric.**

8 As you work down the apple keep referring to the original design so that you know which colours to put where. Although no area is worked in a single colour, you will see that there are areas that are worked primarily in one colour (**G**).

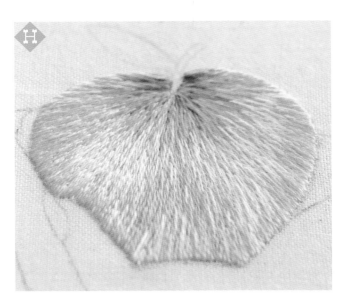

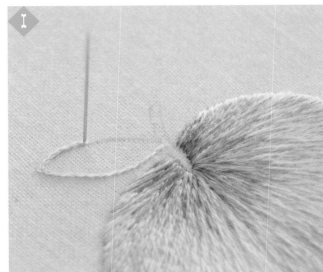

9 Once you've completed the body of the apple (⬦), you need to work the leaf. First do a split stitch around the outside of the leaf (⬦) and then shade it using the dark green and light green colours. Work the leaf in these same colours.

10 To finish off the apple, do a split stitch around the stem and again fill this in with the dark green and light green colours (⬦).

TRICK! Sometimes when you reach the end of a silk shading project you may find that some areas aren't as blended as you wish. One of the great things about this technique is it's very forgiving. You don't want to over work an area but you can always add a few stitches here and there to achieve a more blended effect.

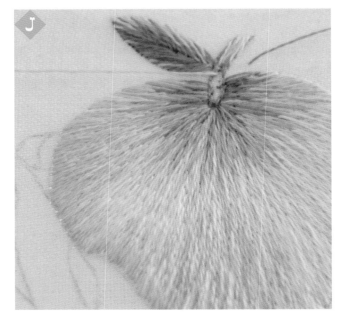

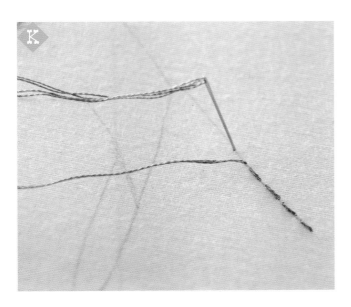

11 Now you need to do the **running stitch** (see 'Stitch Glossary' on page 28) around the hand and sleeve. This is done using two strands of the grey cotton (**K**).

> **TRICK!** Although running stitch is one of the simplest of stitches, it's very effective and really shows off your beautifully worked apple.

12 As you work the running stitch, be aware of the back of your work. If you have any dark threads travelling across the back of your work, you may well see them through the fabric on the front. When you need to jump to another area, weave through your stitches on the back of your work and then continue stitching (**L**) until you have completed the outline of the hand and sleeve (**M**).

Your design is ready to frame, as shown in 'Finishing Techniques' on pages 152–154.

Make it your own!

Mount and frame this piece in a gorgeous, ornate silver frame for full effect, or you can even make it into a cushion or a ring pillow for a wedding.

***

Kissing Couple

LOVE – IT DRAWS YOU INTO ITS EMBRACE AND BRINGS
YOU CLOSE TO THE OBJECT OF YOUR AFFECTION, BUT YOU
MAY ALWAYS WONDER... WILL WE PART?

NOW THAT YOU have learnt the rules of silk shading, let's throw them all out of the window and really paint with the needle. Don't be afraid to go for it on this project and let your stitching flow.

This design uses spotted cotton fabric but you can choose plain, coloured or patterned fabric. The important thing is that the fabric is heavy enough to withstand the dense stitching, so be sure to choose a medium-to-heavyweight fabric.

Finished size:
girl: 3½ x 3⅓ in (9 x 8.5cm);
boy: 3½ in (9cm) square.

Materials

Cotton fabric
12in (30cm) square

**Anchor stranded cotton,
1 skein of each in the
following colours (available
in skeins of 27yd (25m):**

11, 295, 298, 336, 337, 349, 351,
352, 360, 778, 850, 851, 873,
880, 882

Curtains
Single or 1 pair

Equipment

8in (20cm) ring frame

Sharp pair of scissors

Small needles (size 12 or as small as you can manage)

Small screwdriver

Quilter's pencil (optional)

Light box (optional)

Pencil (optional)

112

Instructions

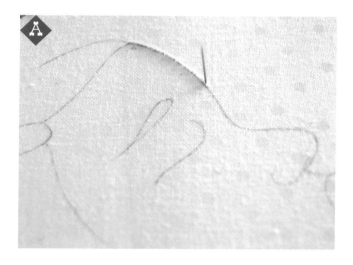

1 Photocopy the design a few times so you have extra copies to make notes on as you go along. You may also find it useful to do a shaded copy in pencil, as this helps to visualize where the light and dark areas are.

2 Put the fabric in the ring frame and pull it as tight as you can, tightening up the screw with a small screwdriver as you go. Trace the design on to your fabric – first the girl, then the boy. If you have any difficulty seeing the design through the fabric, use a light box (if you have one) or tape the design on to the window with the fabric over the top.

3 Use a quilter's pencil to draw on the design so that the lines don't smudge. This is especially important with silk shading as normal pencils can easily rub off and make your threads dirty.

4 First you need to do a **split stitch** (see 'Stitch Glossary' on page 28 and also Step 3 of the *Golden Apple* project on page 105) edge along the outline of the face (**A**).

5 Start at the top of the forehead and work down towards the nose, taking into consideration that the hair would throw a shadow on the face, so the areas of the face next to the hair should be the darker flesh colours (**B**).

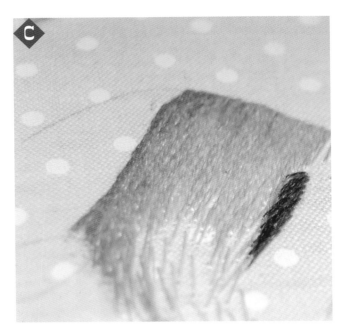

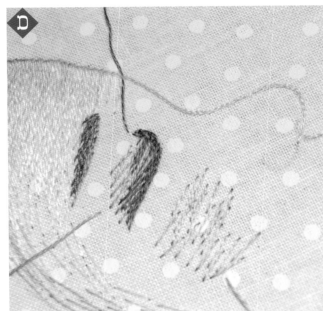

6 As you work down the edge of the face, add in the eyebrow (**C**). Now consider the eye area. For both the boy and the girl, you can use a split stitch to create the line of the eye (use blue for the girl and brown for the boy), then work the eyelids (**D**).

7 Once you've worked the area under the eye, work the eyelashes in the darkest brown colour. Now work the cheeks in the darker flesh tones, giving them a rosy appearance (**E**).

TRICK! You can work areas in the primary colour (for example, the darkest flesh tone under the hair), leaving gaps in between your stitches and then go back and fill in with blending colours.

8 For the nose, do a split stitch around the curve of the nose first, as this clearly differentiates where the nose ends and the cheek starts.

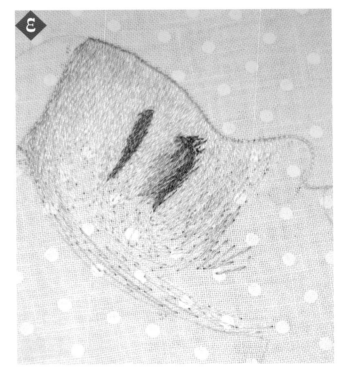

114

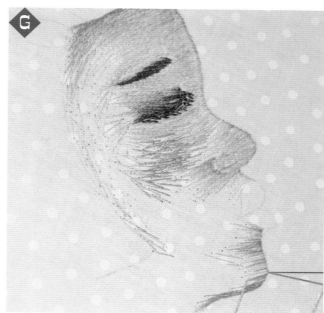

9 Continue working down the face, missing out the lips and carrying on down the chin (**F**) (**G**).

TRICK! For this project, you need to decide quite early on where to stop stitching, and it is a good idea to first visualize the areas you want to leave open.

10 Once you have worked the area around the lips, do a split stitch around them and on the line down the middle of the lips. This is because you want the lips to have a clean neat edge.

11 Work the lips primarily in the rosy pink colour for the girl, and the darkest flesh tone for the boy (**H**).

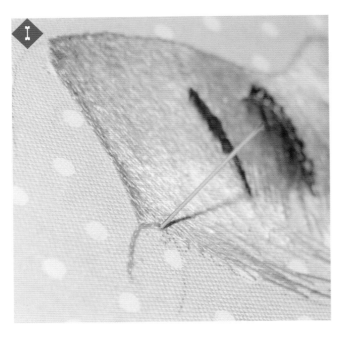

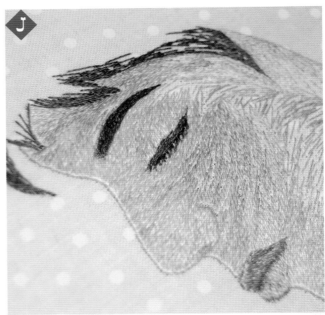

12 For the girl, work a split stitch around the hair band before filling it in with the two yellow colours (◆ **I**).

13 Now work the hair freely. For the girl, also use a little of the blues and purple to add highlights. For the boy, use all of the brown colours (◆ **J**).

14 *Et voila!* A beautiful kissing couple! (◆ **K**)

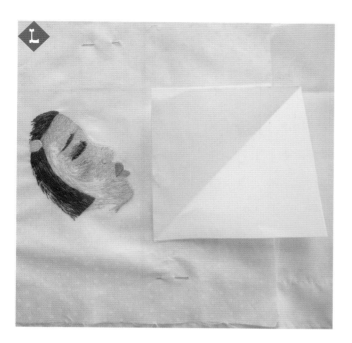

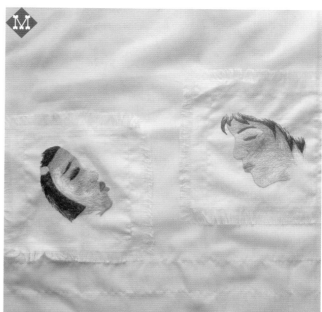

15 In preparation for stitching the faces on to the curtains, first cut a square of paper to use as a stitching guide. The square should clear the finished design all round (**L**).

16 Pin the stitched piece to a fine curtain so that the weave of your fabric lies in the same direction as the weave of the curtain. Centre the paper pattern over the face and stitch using the square as a guide. Trim your stitched piece so that it has a border of approx 1in (2.5cm) and fray the edges.

17 Machine stitch or **back stitch** (see 'Stitch Glossary' on page 26) the girl's face to the bottom left edge of the curtain and then repeat the process with the boy's face, positioning it a short distance away and slightly higher. When the curtain is hung, the folds should create a kissing effect (**M**). You may want to attach each face to a separate curtain to create the same effect.

Make it your own!

Why don't you do your own design of you and your partner or two of your friends? Using a photograph of the faces in profile, trace off the outlines and colour it in with coloured pencils. You can even use this method for a famous couple, pets, comedy duos or favourite film characters.

***

Bird in Flight

BIRDS HAVE LONG BEEN THOUGHT OF AS A LINK BETWEEN MERE MORTALS AND THE HEAVENS ABOVE. THIS DESIGN WILL SNEAK YOU FAR AWAY FROM EARTHLY CONCERNS, TO THE BEAUTY AND IRIDESCENCE OF A BIRD SPREADING ITS WINGS.

WITH ITS USE OF SILK threads on a silk-striped evening skirt, this project is pure luxury both to work and to view, and the spray of Swarovski crystals in the bird's wake creates a stunning effect.

Many people prefer to use stranded cotton for silk shading. Keep in mind, however, that silk behaves differently to cotton – it is slippery and more difficult to control. If you take your time on this project and get used to the silky thread, this sumptuous piece will be a family heirloom for years to come.

Finished size of design: 4⅛ x 5⅛in (10.5 x 13cm).

Materials

Fabric or an item of clothing (a medium to heavy-weight silk or cotton to withstand the dense stitching)

Pearsall's 6-ply filoselle silk – 1 skein of each of the following:

Dull Peacock 117
Silver Grey 143
Silver Grey 146
China Blue 205
China Blue 206
China Blue 208
China Blue 209
Chocolate 213

Pounce

Paint

Swarovski crystals or beads (optional)

Equipment

8in (20cm) ring frame

Sharp pair of scissors

Small needles (size 12 or as small as you can manage)

Small screwdriver

Pricking, pouncing and painting equipment (see page 19 for information)

Pins

118

Instructions

1 Photocopy the design a few times so you have extra copies to make notes on as you go along. Cut the bird out of one of your plain paper copies and pin it on to the fabric where you would like the design to be (**A**).

TRICK! If you're working on a skirt or other garment you may find it useful to place the design while someone is wearing the item, or – if you have one – put the item on a dressmaker's dummy and then pin the design on.

2 Put the fabric with the pinned design in the ring frame and pull it as tight as you can, tightening up the screw with a small screwdriver as you go and being careful to ensure the bird is central in the frame (**B**).

3 Transfer the design using the 'Pricking, Pouncing and Painting' technique – see 'Basic Techniques' on page 19 (**C**).

4 Once the design has been transferred, you need to do a **split stitch** (see 'Stitch Glossary' on page 28 and also see Step 3 of the *Golden Apple* project on page 105) around the body of the bird in one of the medium blue colours. Split stitch just on the outside edge of your design line to avoid it showing and use one strand of silk. Always do the split stitch in one of the main colours you are going to shade with, just in case a little peep shows through when you come to stitch over it (**D**).

5 Start your shading in the darkest blue colour at the beak. Always begin with a stitch in the centre of your shape, bringing your needle up in the shape and down over the outside edge, then continue working outwards from this stitch. Your smallest stitches should be no smaller than $\frac{1}{8}$in (3mm) and no larger than $\frac{3}{8}$in (1cm). It may feel at first like your stitches are unnaturally long but don't worry about that as when you come to do your second row you will be coming up in the stitches of this first row and will therefore lose some of the length (**E**).

TRICK! Work along the row in one colour, leaving gaps in between your stitches to get the stitch direction correct, but also so you can go back and fill in with another colour.

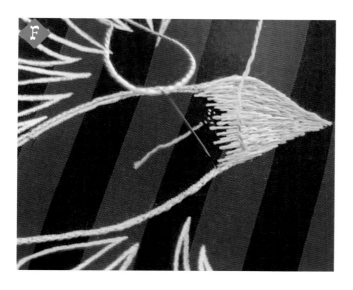

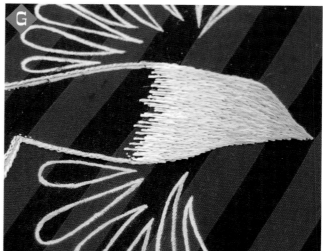

6 For your second row, bring the needle up in the stitches of your first row, and take the needle down directly into the fabric. Use the full length of the stitches of the first row, bringing some of your stitches really quite close up to the edge and others much further down (**F**).

7 The colours on the bird's body graduate from the dark to the lightest blue, then light and dark grey and a little of the coral colour towards the tail. You will need to change colours roughly every two or three rows, and be mindful to blend the two colours together where they meet (**G**).

8 Continue working down the body, being careful to cover all of the fabric with your stitching as you go. On the edges, keep your stitches long as you cover the split stitch – don't be tempted to angle your stitches outwards too much (**H**).

9 Once you've completed the body, you can work the wings. First you need to split stitch around the edges of the wings, in whatever colour blue you are using on that wing. You can split stitch around all of the wing sections and then do the silk shading, or you can work each wing to completion one by one (◆I◆). You can also work them by colour, doing the same colours on both sides before moving on to the next colour (◆J◆).

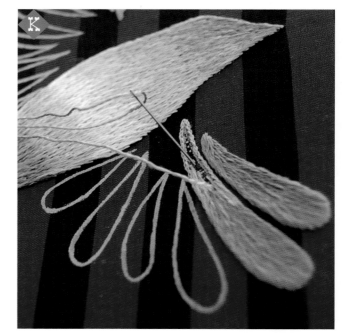

10 If filling one wing at a time, start the silk shading at the tip of the bird's wings, first with the coral and then work down the shape. Introduce the blue around half way down and graduate through the blue shades from section to section (◆K◆).

11 You now need to work the tail feathers, again with the coral colour at the tips and working in to blue then grey to meet with the body ().

TRICK! Sometimes when you reach the end of a silk shading project you may find that some areas aren't as blended as you wish. One of the great things about this technique is it's very forgiving. You don't want to over work an area but you can always add a few stitches here and there to achieve a more blended effect.

12 Now that the bird itself is complete, you can add any number of Swarovski crystals, or any other type of beads or stones, in its wake (🔵).

Make it your own!

This design could have many uses – it would look stunning on the back of a blazer, and would work equally well as a cushion or a framed piece (see 'Finishing Techniques', pages 152–158 for instructions). Choose your own colours and don't be afraid to embellish the area around it, to really bring the bird to life.

CHAPTER 4

Goldwork

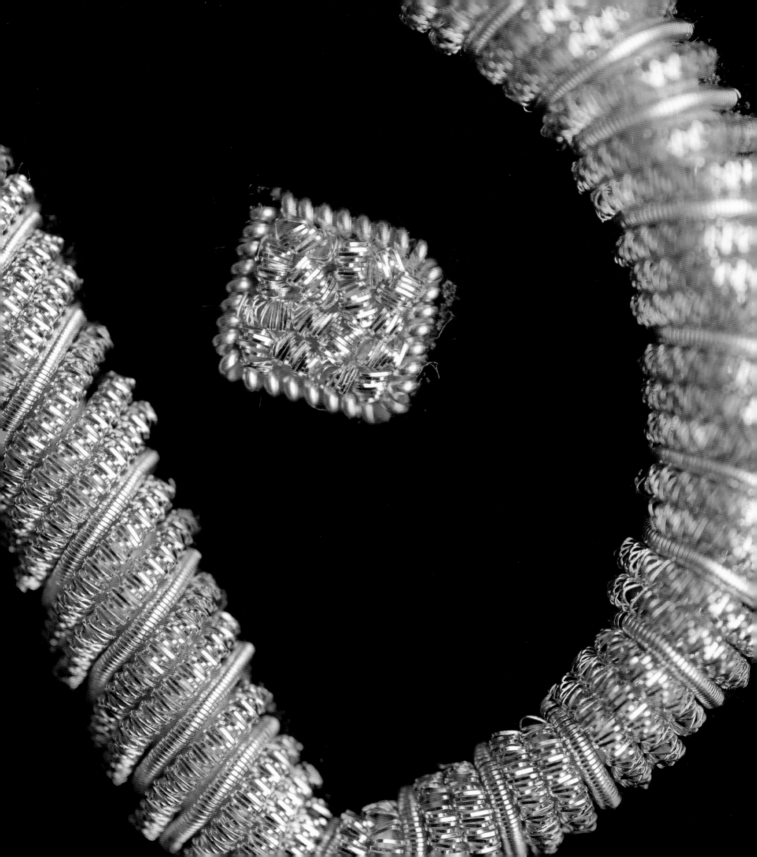

GOLDWORK

ORIGINATING IN ASIA AT LEAST 2,000 YEARS AGO, GOLDWORK HAS BEEN MOST WIDELY KNOWN FOR ITS USE IN ECCLESIASTICAL WORK, TO CREATE STRIKING BANNERS, VESTMENTS AND ALTAR FRONTALS.

IN THE MIDDLE AGES, a style using goldwork, called Opus Anglicanum, was developed in England and used in church vestments and hangings. Soon after, it became common to adorn the clothing and furnishings of royalty with goldwork. In England, it's traditional for goldwork to be raised and an excellent example of this is the Queen's Coronation robes, which were embroidered at the Royal School of Needlework. Felt, carpet felt or soft string padding can be used to create a raised effect and the gold threads are applied on top of the padding.

128

Despite its name, goldwork includes the art of working with all metal threads, not just those that are gold. While it is incredibly striking, as the light plays on the sumptuous threads, this stunning effect often acts as a deterrent for even the most experienced stitchers, who believe it is too difficult. Yet goldwork only uses two methods of stitching – couching over or sewing through as you would a bead – not nearly as complicated as many people think!

However, one of the down sides of using metal threads is that they are very delicate and therefore cannot be washed and must be handled carefully. This means that this technique is unsuitable for cushions and clothing, but perfect for framed pictures or items of jewellery.

THE PROJECTS

In this chapter you will find three projects. The first project, the *Winged Brooch*, also employs appliqué and stumpwork (or raised embroidery) techniques. If you feel a little nervous about having a go at goldwork, start with this project, as the principles are very simple. The *Ferris Wheel* picture teaches you the basics of padding and also how to do couching and chipping, and the last project – the *Drama* picture – aims to be just that… dramatic! This project uses cutwork, a technique where you have to cut each piece of gold to fit over your padding before you sew through it like a bead. This can be fiddly to begin with, but remain patient and you will get the hang of it!

Opposite: Goldwork Crown by **Sophie Long**
Top left: Disco Daisy by **Nicola Jarvis**
Top right: Hand-embroidered brooches by **Jenny Adin Christie**
Above: Pyramid Box by **Jenny Adin Christie**

Winged Brooch

WINGS SYMBOLIZE FLIGHT BUT ALSO PEACE AND LOVE.

IMMERSE YOURSELF IN MAKING THIS STUNNING BROOCH

FOR YOUR OWN CREATIVE 'ESCAPE'.

EMBROIDERY DOESN'T HAVE to be flat. It can become three dimensional with the simple use of wire.

Raised embroidery techniques, also known as stumpwork, are used here to achieve this impressive three-dimensional effect, and the appliquéd heart and sumptuous spangles will give this brooch instant impact.

This brooch can be made to adorn your favourite top, jacket or even a handbag, or you could give it as a gift to someone special in your life.

Finished size: 2³⁄₄ x 3in (7.5 x 7cm).

Materials

Medium calico
12in (30cm) square

Paper-covered cake wire
4 lengths

Red variegated stranded cotton • 1 skein

Red felt
4in (10cm) square

Red silk
4in (10cm) square

Iron-on transfer adhesive
4in (10cm) square

Gilt no. 1 pearl purl
1¹⁄₂in (4cm) length

Yellow machine thread
1 reel

Spangles
2 sizes, approximately 200

Brooch back • 1 piece

Wax • 1 small block

Equipment

8in (20cm) ring frame

Sharp pair of scissors

Small screwdriver

Paper scissors

Needles

Pliers

Pencil

Mellor (optional)

Quilter's pencil (optional)

Light box (optional)

Mini iron (optional)

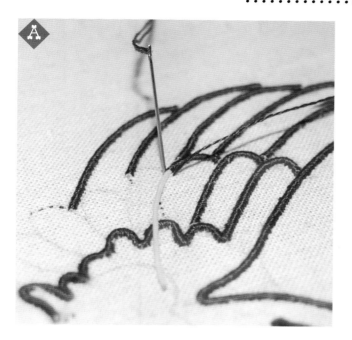

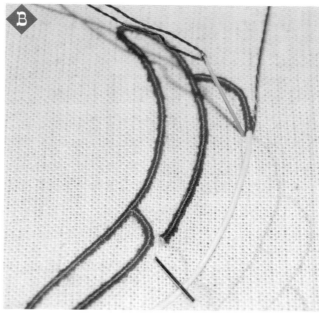

1 Photocopy the design a few times so you have extra copies to cut up and make notes on as you go through the project.

2 Trace the design on to the calico. If you have any difficulty seeing the design through the fabric, use a light box (if you have one) or tape the design on to the window, placing the fabric over the top. A quilter's pencil can be very useful for drawing on designs, as the lines don't smudge. Put the fabric in the ring frame and pull the fabric as tight as you can, tightening up the screw with a small screwdriver as you go.

3 First you need to do the **trailing** (see 'Stitch Glossary' on page 29) to give your brooch a solid form. Stitch paper-covered wire down using one strand of stranded cotton. A variegated thread has been used here but you can use any colour you like. Start by catching down the end of the wire with your first stitch, and then work along it, bringing the needle up on one side of the wire and taking it down on the other. Keep your stitches really close together so that none of the wire is showing through (**A**). You will also need to bend and manipulate the wire to fit the shapes (**B**). A pair of pliers can be helpful for this.

TRICK! Angle your needle outwards as you bring it up, and inwards as you take it down to make your stitches really tight. This will make it easier when you come to cutting out your brooch, as you're less likely to cut any of your stitches.

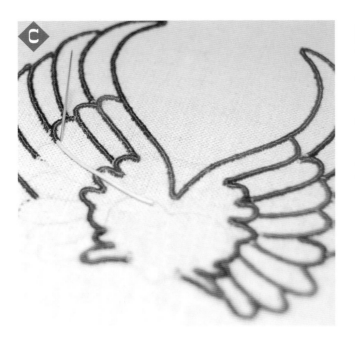

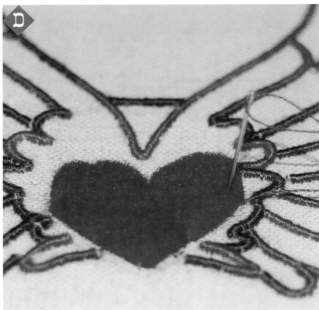

4 Work the whole design in trailing, with the exception of the heart (**C**).

TRICK! Be mindful of the threads going across the back of your work. Make sure all threads remain within the shape of the design, otherwise you will cut them when you come to cut out your brooch later on.

5 Cut the heart shape out of one of your paper copies of the design. Pin it onto the red felt and cut out two heart shapes.

6 Trim one of the heart shapes down so it fits inside the other, and stitch down the smaller heart using **stab stitch** (see the *One* project on page 94 for another example of applying fabric using stab stitch, or see 'Stitch Glossary' on page 28). Apply the second heart over the top (**D**).

7 Now you can apply the red silk. To avoid fraying, trace and then cut out the heart shape in iron-on adhesive and iron this on to the silk. In turn, cut the silk heart shape out and iron it on to the felt before stab stitching around the edge. For further information on applying iron-on adhesive, see the *One* project on page 93.

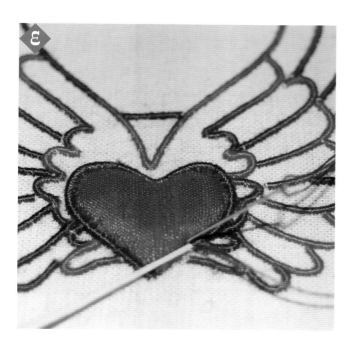

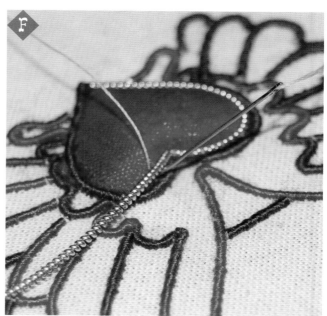

8 Once the silk heart is securely sewn down, stitch trailing around the outside edge of the heart, covering your stab stitches as you go – again, this was done with variegated thread (**E**).

9 Now you need to stitch down the pearl purl around the inside edge of the trailing. Pearl purl is a metal thread that, when stretched, looks like a spring. Before you start, stretch it a tiny bit to open out the grooves and make room for your stitches.

10 Start at the point of the heart and, with your first stitch, catch down the first groove of the pearl purl. Do a stitch every two or three grooves, bending the pearl purl round to fit the shape as you go (**F**).

11 When you reach the point of the heart again, cut any excess pearl purl away and, again, catch down the last groove with your final stitch (**G**).

12 Now comes the fun bit – stitching down the spangles! This design uses two sizes of spangles to fill the shapes completely but you can use as few or as many as you like. Stitch them down using **back stitch** (see 'Stitch Glossary' on page 26). This means you come up at the bottom of a shape, thread on a spangle and then take the needle down behind it. You then bring your needle up in front of the spangle, thread on the next one and take your needle down in the hole of the previous spangle. Continue in this way until the shape has been filled (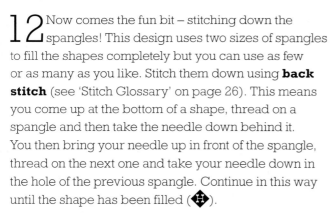).

TRICK! Wax your thread before stitching down the spangles. This gives the thread grip, which keeps the spangles in place.

13 With all the stitching done, you can cut your brooch out. First leave an excess of calico, and then cut it away gradually and carefully, being certain not to cut any of your stitches. Once you've cut all the calico away, rub a pin along the edge of your brooch to free any loose threads, and then trim away (◆).

14 Stitch a brooch back on behind the heart shape and then bend and manipulate your brooch into the shape you want it to be.

Make it your own!

Use different-coloured sequins, or even adorn this design with beads. You can make a brooch of any shape using this technique – the important thing is that it's solid. Use trailing around all edges, do lots of embellishment and, for added strength, apply felt to the back of the brooch and stitch it in place.

Ferris Wheel

THIS FUN AND EASY-TO-MAKE DESIGN WILL TAKE YOU STRAIGHT

BACK TO ALL THE EXCITING AND ROMANTIC THRILLS OF THE FAIRGROUND.

HOLD HANDS AND TAKE TO THE SKIES...

IN DREAMS, the Ferris wheel can represent the circle of life, and the ups and downs we all face on our own exciting journeys through it. The circle also points to the centre of our personalities, with spokes radiating out into the wider world.

The beautiful, postcard-sized embroidery is stitched in sumptuous silver and copper threads to give it twinkle and shine. The painted blue sky and clouds adds a creative twist on traditional stitching, with space for you to personalize it if you wish by stitching your favourite quote over the sky. It's a true piece of art and certainly one to hang in pride of place.

Finished size of design: 5¾ x 4in (14.8 x 10.5cm).

Materials

Natural linen
15in (38cm) square

White felt • 4in (10cm) square

Blue machine thread
(for tacking) • 1 reel

Grey machine thread • 1 reel

Copper machine thread
1 reel

Silver Japanese thread
2¼ yd (2m)

Silver ophir thread • 1 reel

Copper pearl purl • 2 grams

Silver bright check • 2.5 grams

Blue watercolour paint
1 small tube

White watercolour paint
1 small tube

Wax • 1 small block

Equipment

10in (25cm) ring frame

Sharp pair of scissors

Needles

Small screwdriver

Paper scissors

Paint brushes

Pencil

Pins

Mellor (optional)

Stiletto (optional)

Light box (optional)

Quilter's pencil (optional)

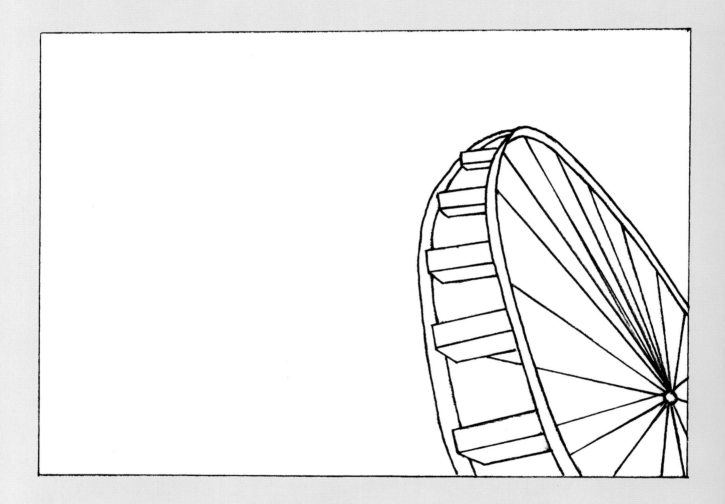

Instructions

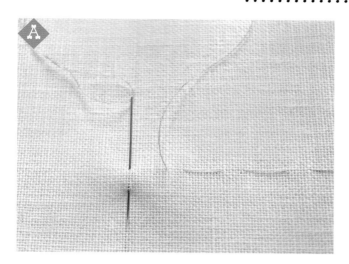

1 Photocopy the design a few times so you have extra copies to cut up and make notes on as you go through the project. Lay the linen over the design and tack on the boundary line using a **running stitch** (see 'Stitch Glossary' on page 28) (**A**). This will help you keep the design the right size, and will come in handy when mounting your piece.

2 Trace the design on to the linen (a quilter's pencil is the best thing for this as the lines won't smudge). If you have any difficulty seeing the design through the fabric, use a light box (if you have one) or tape the design on to the window, with the fabric over the top (**B**).

3 Put the fabric in the ring frame and pull the fabric as tight as you can, tightening up the screw with a small screwdriver as you go.

4 Now you need to cut out the padding. Cut the edges of the Ferris wheel, the carriages and the small circle in the middle out of one of your paper copies. Lay or pin the shapes on to the white felt and cut them out one by one. For the carriages, you will need to do two layers of felt, so cut two pieces of felt out for each carriage, and then cut one down so it's a little smaller than the other.

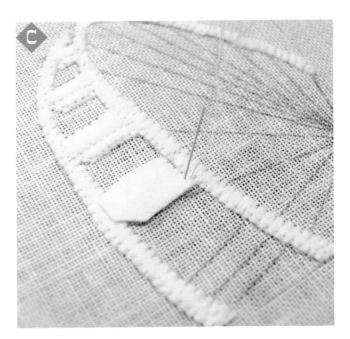

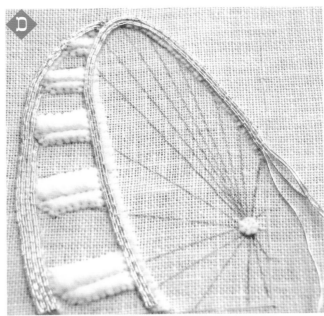

5 The smaller shape gets stitched down first. The edges of the wheel and the small circle require only one layer of felt. Stitch down the pieces using a **stab stitch** (see 'Stitch Glossary' on page 28), bringing your needle up on the outside of the shape and down in the felt (◆).

6 Once all the felt has been securely stitched down, you can begin **couching** (see 'Stitch Glossary' on page 26) over the Japanese thread. This involves Japanese thread being laid on the top of the fabric and you stitch over two lengths of it together. To start off, take a length of Japanese thread and fold it in half. Using a single length of waxed grey machine thread, do one stitch over the folded end of the Japanese thread, then do a stitch over the two lengths together

and continue up the thread in this way, keeping your stitches at right angles with approximately a 1/8in (3mm) gap between your stitches. When you reach the end of the shape, leave the excess Japanese thread hanging. These ends will be plunged through the fabric later.

7 When you come to do your second row, start again in exactly the same way. As you work up the thread, **brick** (see 'Stitch Glossary' on page 26) your stitches so they sit in between the stitches of your first row (◆).

8 Once the areas have been filled with couching, you will need to plunge the ends through to the back of the fabric and secure them.

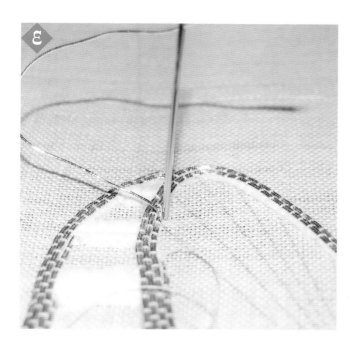

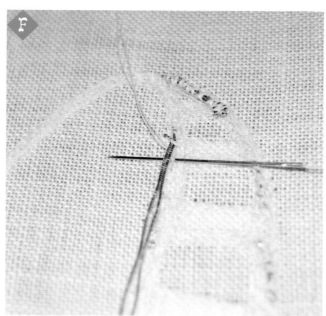

9 Cut the strands of Japanese thread down to about 2in (5cm) and make a small hole in the fabric where the end needs to be plunged – you can do this using a stiletto if you have one, or a large needle (⬥E).

10 Thread the end of the Japanese thread on to a large needle and pull it through to the back. Always plunge the ends one by one and tie off the ends once all of them have been plunged.

11 To secure the ends of the Japanese thread, turn the ring frame over to the back and, using a double length of waxed thread, stitch over the threads two at a time until you feel that they are secure (⬥F).

TRICK! Always tie back the ends behind an area that has already been worked so that they don't get in your way.

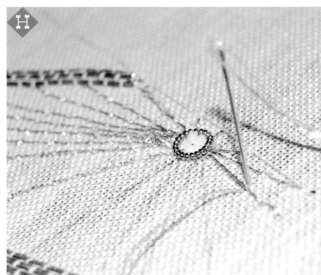

12 Now you need to stitch down the copper pearl purl that outlines the carriages. Pearl purl is made completely of metal and therefore there are no ends to unravel and it sits entirely on top of the fabric. Pearl purl is like a tightly woven spring and your stitches sit in the grooves of the thread. Cut a small piece, approximately 3in (8cm) long, grab each end between your thumb and forefinger and very gently stretch it out a little. This gives the space between the grooves for your stitches to sit in.

13 Trim the end of the pearl purl and, using a single waxed length of copper machine thread, stitch down the first groove of the pearl purl in one of the corners of the largest carriage. Continue couching over the pearl purl, doing a stitch every two or three grooves. When you reach the corners,

bend the pearl purl back on itself to create a sharp point. Stitch around the outside edge of the carriage and then stitch the line across the carriage. Work all of the carriages and also around the edge of the small circle in the middle of the wheel (**G**).

TRICK! If you have a mellor or laying tool, use it to manipulate the thread and straighten the lines.

14 Now you can stitch the lines on the wheel in single thread couching using a single length of silver ophir thread. Bring your needle up next to the circle in the centre and take it down at the far edge of the wheel. Work back down the thread, couching it down as you go. When you reach the centre, repeat this for the next line and so on (**H**).

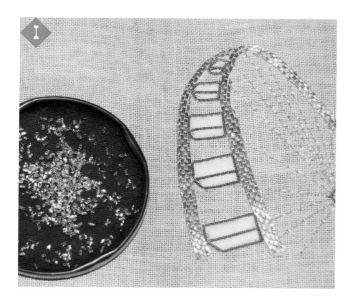

15 You can now work the chips in the carriages and circle using the silver bright check thread. This thread comes in lengths and is hollow, so you cut it down to the required size and stitch through it as you would a bead. First cut lots of tiny pieces of bright check, no larger than $\frac{1}{16}$ in (1.5mm) each (◆I).

16 Stitch the chips down randomly using a double length of waxed grey thread. The chips should be laying in all different directions on their sides, so you can't see the hollow end (◆J). Continue in this way until all the shapes have been filled.

17 You can now, if you wish, paint your background. This design uses watercolour paint to create the impression of blue sky and clouds. Use blue and white paint mixed together, and quite watered down to begin with, to create a wash. Build up the colour and shapes of clouds gradually. (◆K)

Your design is ready to frame, as shown in 'Finishing Techniques' on pages 152–154.

Make it your own!

Instead of painting the background, you could stitch a favourite quote, or if it's a gift, a personal message. You don't have to use silver and copper – there are lots of coloured metal threads available.

***

Drama

GOLDWORK, BY NATURE, IS QUITE A THEATRICAL TECHNIQUE.
THIS CHEEKY DESIGN CAPTURES THIS WITH A FLOURISH,
USING SUMPTUOUS GOLD THREADS ON LUXURIOUS PURPLE VELVET.

TO CREATE the three-dimensional effect, the letters are padded first and cutwork is applied over the top. This spectacular piece would look perfect in a living room or – if you're lucky enough to have one – in a dressing room.

This is the only project in the book that uses a slate frame (see 'Basic Techniques', pages 24–25). Slate frames can be expensive and take time to prepare, as your fabric is sewn in to it, but if you want to do larger projects or lots of embroidery, it is worth buying one – they make working much easier and more comfortable, plus they keep your fabric really tight, which avoids any puckering. If you don't want to use a slate frame, simply reduce the size of the design a little and use a 10in (25cm) ring frame.

Finished size of design: 6½ x 7in (18 x 16.5cm).

Materials

Purple velvet
15 x 10in (38 x 25cm)

Calico
18in (46cm) square to fit 18in (46cm) square slate frame

Soft string
33ft (10m)

Machine thread
1 reel

Gilt smooth
4 grams

Gilt bright check
4 grams

Gilt Pearl purl
½ gram

Wax
1 small block

Pounce

Paint

Equipment

Tracing paper

Pricking, pouncing and painting equipment
(see page 19)

Small paintbrush

18in (46cm) slate frame

Sharp pair of scissors

Needles

Mellor/laying tool (optional)

DRAMA

ADVENTURES IN NEEDLEWORK

Instructions

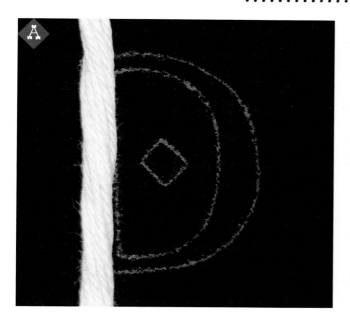

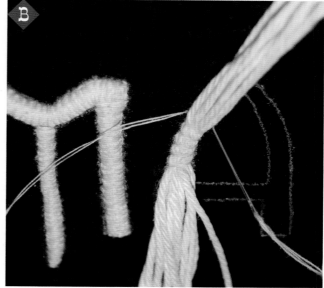

1 Photocopy the design a few times so you have extra copies to cut up and make notes on as you go through the project. Put the fabric in your chosen frame and transfer the design (see Pricking and Pouncing in 'Basic Techniques' on page 19).

2 Now you can work the padding, done using soft string. Think of each letter in sections, for example, the 'D' has two sections: the straight part and the curved part. Hold the soft string in your hand and, about 5in (12.5cm) down, turn it back on itself. Continue doing this until you have around 10 strands of the string together (but don't cut the string yet). Twist it and lay it on to the first section of the letter to see if it will fit inside the design, if there are too many of too few strands, just add some or take some away (**A**).

3 You then need to wax the string (see 'Materials and Equipment', page 16). Do this a few times before winding the string together again, then pull it through the wax a few more times. When you hold one end of it, it should be able to stand up of its own accord.

4 Lay the string onto the velvet and, with a double strand of machine thread, start stitching the string down from the centre of the shape. Bring your needle up on one side, take it down on the other and pull your stitches tight. The neatness of your stitches doesn't matter so much at this stage – what's important is to mould the string into the shapes of the letters (**B**).

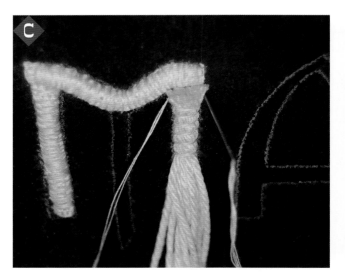

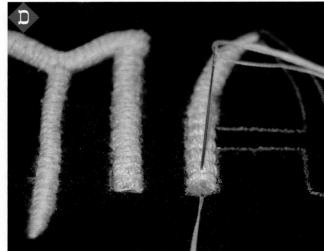

5 Where a shape tapers out, cut away the strands of the string gradually, separating them off from underneath the others and cutting away as you go. Where a shape ends abruptly, cut away any excess at the end of the shape and stitch down securely, catching down any fluffy ends (**C**)(**D**).

6 Cut a small diamond shape out of yellow felt and **stab stitch** (see 'Stitch Glossary' on page 28) it down in the centre of the 'D' (**E**).

> **TRICK!** When you start, put one end of your machine thread through the needle, pull it through so the two ends of your threads meet and tie a knot in them. This way you can easily pull the pieces of gold off the thread, as you don't have a loose end getting in the way.

7 Now you can begin the cutwork. Always start in the centre of the section you are working and in this case, use a double length of waxed machine thread. This design uses two or three pieces of bright check to every one piece of smooth purl, but you can do any combination you like. Where you're

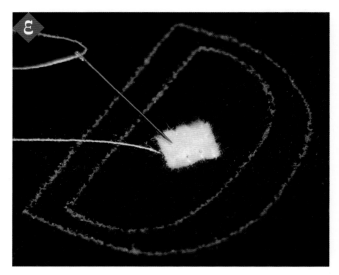

working a regular shape, use your first piece of gold as a measure to cut a few more. That way you'll know they're the correct length.

> **TRICK!** Put your gold threads on a square of felt on or next to your frame. This stops them from pinging away as you cut and work with them. You can also use a velvet board for this if you have one.

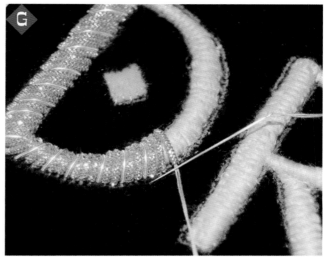

8 Cut your first piece of gold a little longer than it needs to be, thread it on and, using your needle, push it in to place to see if it fits. If it's a little too short, take it off your thread and cut another piece. If it's too long, simply cut a little off. Velvet is very forgiving, as the pile gives you a little room for error, but ultimately you want your gold to cover the shape without buckling and without the thread showing (◆). This will seem fiddly initially but persevere and you'll soon get the knack of cutting the gold to the right length.

9 Use a mellor, also known as a laying tool, (see 'Materials and Equipment', page 17) to lay down the gold and manipulate it in to place. You can also use your needle to hold and move the pieces (◆).

TRICK! As you work, cover up completed areas with tissue paper and bubble wrap to avoid damage.

10 Once you've completed all the cutwork, stitch pearl purl around the diamond edge, then cut tiny chips of bright check and stitch them down randomly to fill the shape. (See page 145, steps 15 and 16 for more information on chipping.)

TRICK! Velvet attracts fluff. If you need to, you can clean it at the end with a little transparent tape, being careful not to catch the gold.

Your design is ready to frame, as shown in 'Finishing Techniques' on pages 152–154.

Make it your own!

Choose your own typeface or work a different word or name entirely, perhaps that of a family member, beloved pet or surname. You can even use your own nickname, if you have one…

FINISHING TECHNIQUES

ONCE YOU'VE COMPLETED a project, you will more than likely want to make it into something. You may wish to mount it ready for framing or make it in to a cushion, handbag or wall hanging. There is so much joy to be found in finishing your project, whether it is to be a decorative or practical item.

If you notice that your canvaswork is slightly warped or pulled to one side, which can happen if a piece is worked without a frame, you can do what is known as 'blocking'. Simply spray your work lightly on both sides with clean or distilled water so that it is damp but not soaking. Transfer your work to a towel or blotting paper and blot. Lay your work on a clean, dry surface and gently pull so that the corners are 90 degrees and the sides are straight. Dry flat.

Mounting a project for framing

This is the traditional way of finishing a project and although it takes a while it really is worth spending time on to ensure your work is finished beautifully and survives for future generations. Any kind of adhesive can damage your work over time, and this technique means that no glue whatsoever touches your project. If you intend to frame your work, purchase the frame first and mount your piece to fit the frame.

MATERIALS AND EQUIPMENT

Your finished needlework design
Acid-free mount board
Strong white glue
Medium-weight cotton calico
Buttonhole thread
Curved needle
Cotton sateen (optional)

INSTRUCTIONS

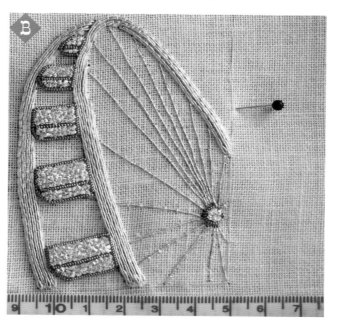

1 Decide what you would like the finished size of your project to be and cut two pieces of acid-free mount board to the final size of your project. Stick them together with strong white glue, then put the card on to a piece of calico and cut around it, leaving approximately 1½in (4cm) excess fabric around the edges. Put strong white glue down one side of the card, turn the calico over the edge of the card and stick it down. Turn the card round and do the same on the opposite side.

2 You now need to cut the excess fabric away from the corners. Cut at an angle with the point of your scissors going into the corner. Once you've done all four corners, turn the other two sides over and stick them down.

3 Using a tape measure, mark the centre of the four sides of your fabric-covered card with a pencil (**A**). Place your finished project on to your card and pin in place at the four side centre points (**B**).

4 From the centre working outwards, pin along one of the edges then pull the fabric from the opposite side and pin that edge. Do the same with the last two edges, pulling the fabric as tight as possible as you go and manipulating it so the grain of your fabric is straight (look out for this particularly on the corners) (**C**).

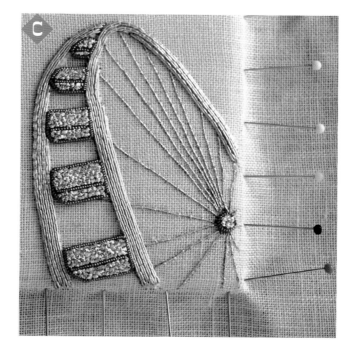

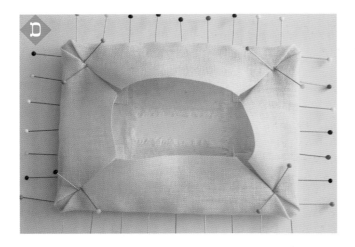

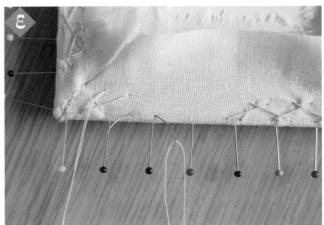

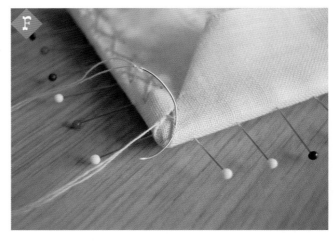

5 Turn the piece over, then turn the corners in and fold the sides over, pinning in place (**D**).

6 Using a double length of buttonhole thread and a curved needle, **herringbone stitch** (see 'Stitch Glossary' on page 27) your project on to the calico (**E**).

7 At the corners, **slip stitch** (see 'Stitch Glossary' on page 28) down into the corner (**F**) and then cut away the excess fabric at the corners.

8 If you wish, you can then place a piece of cotton sateen fabric on to the back of your work, turn the edges under and slip stitch in place.

Make it your own!

There are lots of different frames available: choose mirrored, ornate, plain, wooden and painted frames that you love, or pick a frame to match your décor. If you're not sure which frame to choose, take your project to a framing shop and ask for advice.

Making a cushion

A needlepoint cushion can be made in a variety of ways using different types of fastenings and trimming. Ideally the cushion should be backed in a medium-weight furnishing fabric with a tight weave to prevent fraying. Pure cotton is ideal and easy to work with. The instructions below are for a simple zip-fastened cushion that would be perfect for a rectangular or square cushion such as the *Lean on Me*, *Passion* or *Bargello Sardines* projects in this book.

MATERIALS AND EQUIPMENT

Your finished blocked needlepoint
Medium-weight cotton fabric for backing
Sewing thread to match your cushion
Sewing machine or sewing needle
Pins
Sharp general purpose scissors
Close-ended zipper (measure the depth of your needlework and opt for a zip of the same measurement)
Tape measure

INSTRUCTIONS

1 Trim your needlepoint design, leaving a seam allowance all around the finished piece of ⅝in (1.5cm). Your backing fabric will need to be cut in two halves. The depth of each half is the depth of your needlepoint plus the 1¼in (3cm) seam allowances. The width of each half is half the width of your needlepoint plus 1¼in (3cm) to allow for two seam allowances.

2 With right sides together, pin what will be the centre point of your cushion backing. Stitch a ⅝in (1.5cm) seam 1¼in (3cm) long at the top and bottom edge of the fabric. Using long stitches, join the gap between the seams, stitching along the seam line. Open out the fabric and the seam allowances and press (◆).

TRICK! Many fabric cushions incorporate a zipper in one of the side seams. It can be better, however, to place the zipper at the centre back of your cushion. This is because the weight of your needlepoint will inevitably be a different weight, texture and thickness to your backing fabric and aligning both sides of the zip is tricky on different weights of fabric. Another reason for placing a zipper at the back of your cushion is if you choose to machine stitch the zipper tapes in place, machine stitching can ruin the look of your needlepoint.

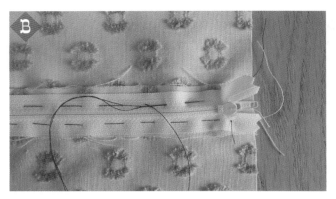

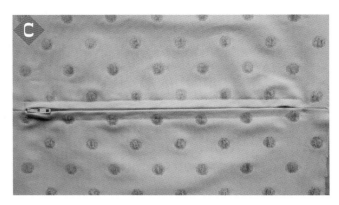

3 Place the open zipper face down over the seam allowances at the back of your backing fabric. The top of the zipper teeth should lie just over the stitching and the zipper teeth should run along the length of your long stitches. Stitch the zipper tape through all layers using long stitches, keeping clear of the zipper teeth. Close the zipper and stitch the remaining tape in the same way (**B**).

4 Turn your backing fabric over and stitch using a zipper attachment on your sewing machine, or by hand using **prick stitch**. Prick stitch is a form of **back stitch** (see 'Stitch Glossary' on page 26), but rather than creating equal-sized stitches both above and below your work, when you bring your needle up, catch only a very few strands of material with your needle and return below, leaving a tiny stitch only. Unpick the long stitches around the zipper tape and at the centre seam to expose your zipper (**C**).

5 With right sides together, place your backing fabric over your needlepoint, matching the edges. If you are using a trimming, sandwich it between the layers, ensuring that the trimming tape will be hidden in the seam allowance and the decorative part will lie on the needlepoint. Machine or back stitch round the entire edge. If you are using a bulky

trimming such as a pom-pom edging and you are machine stitching, you will need to use a zipper foot, as a regular machine foot will not be able to travel over the bulk of the trimming.

6 Trim the corners diagonally, staying away from the stitching, and turn your cushion inside out through the zipper opening. Press through a clean white cotton cloth using a steam iron on a wool setting (**D**).

7 If you want to pipe your cushion and are using a piping without attached binding, **slip stitch** (see 'Stitch Glossary' on page 28) the piping around the edge using invisible or matching coloured thread.

Making a needlepoint bag or purse

Making a purse or bag using a metal frame is not as difficult as it appears, and by following the instructions, no one will believe you made it yourself. It is important to select the type of frame you wish to use before you begin. Metal purse frames come in a variety of shapes, sizes and finishes. Some are suitable for small purses, some large enough to be used for clutch bags. This is the ideal way to make a clutch bag – for more detailed instructions on how to make a bag or purse, see the *Fish Tattoo* bag project on pages 56–63.

MATERIALS AND EQUIPMENT

Your finished needlepoint project
Metal frame
Lining material (100% cotton is best)
Very strong fabric glue
Sewing thread to match your bag
Sewing machine or sewing needle
General all-purpose scissors
Large sheet of brown paper
Indelible pen

INSTRUCTIONS

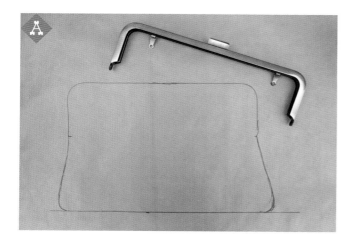

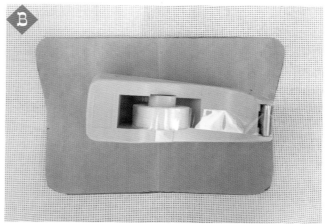

1 Place the purse frame on a large piece of brown paper and draw around the outside of the frame, marking where the hinges join. Now decide what shape you want your purse to be. Angling the side lines of the purse is the best option, as it creates fullness and space in the bag. Draw a line indicating the depth of the bag and round off the bottom corners (**A**).

2 Cut out this shape – this is your template for your finished bag and can be used as a design area for your needlepoint. Weighting down your pattern piece to prevent it from slipping, draw the shape on to your needlepoint canvas or fabric with an indelible pen and flip upside down to form a mirror image. You are now ready to stitch your design onto the canvas (**B**).

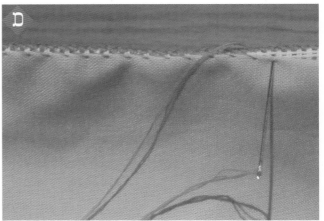

3 Once you have completed your design, cut it out, adding a border of canvas or fabric all the way round to form a seam allowance. Typically, this border should be ⅝in (1.5cm). Using the bag template, mark the hinge positions with an indelible pen.

4 Cut the same shape from your lining material, adding the same amount of fabric as a seam allowance and marking the position of the hinges.

5 With the right sides of your finished needlepoint design together, machine or **back stitch** (see 'Stitch Glossary' on page 26) the sides of the bag from the bottom corners, leaving the seam allowance open above the hinge position. Repeat this process with the lining material. Trim and clip the corners of the outer bag and turn the right way out. Press lightly through a clean cloth (◆).

6 Press the lining and turn the seam allowance over towards the outside. You may need to clip the corners within the seam allowance to accommodate the fullness of fabric. Insert the lining into the bag pocket without turning inside out.

7 Fold the seam allowance of the canvas above the hinge position to the inside. **Slip stitch** (see 'Stitch Glossary' on page 28) the outer bag to the lining (◆).

8 Using the fabric glue, carefully apply it to one side of the inner channel of your frame, starting from one hinge, round to the other. Apply a line of glue to the outer slip-stitched edge of your bag from the area above one hinge position, all the way round to the other hinge position.

9 Carefully insert the bag, placing its sides inside the frame and then pushing in the top. You may need a flat object such as a butter knife to help you poke the bag all the way up so that it reaches the top of the frame. Allow the bag to dry for 30 minutes and then carefully pick off any dry glue that has oozed from the frame on to your needlepoint.

Making a wall hanging

A needlepoint wall hanging is a wonderful and original way to add softness, warmth and texture to a room.

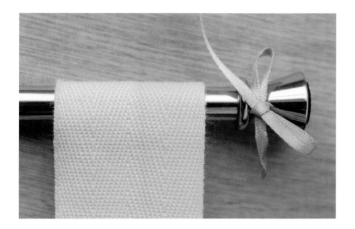

MATERIALS AND EQUIPMENT

Your finished blocked needlepoint
Ribbon, webbing or fabric for loops
   (see left)
Ribbon or cord for hanging
Metal or wooden baton to comfortably house
   the width of your needlepoint
Heavy cotton fabric for backing
Sewing thread to match your wall hanging
Sewing machine or sewing needle
Pins
Fabric scissors
Tape measure

INSTRUCTIONS

1 Trim your needlepoint, leaving a seam allowance all around the finished piece of ⅝in (1.5cm). Cut your backing fabric to the same size.

2 The loops required to hang your needlepoint need to be deep enough for the supporting baton or rod to be inserted. Your needlepoint needs to hang comfortably from these loops, and a little space between the rod and the beginning of the top edge of your wall hanging is often the most aesthetically pleasing. To determine how long you would like your loops to be, you may want to fold the upper edge of your needlepoint over and lay it on the floor. Next, place your baton or rod at the preferred distance above it.

3 Taking a tape measure, measure from the top of your needlework, around the baton or rod and back down to the top of your needlepoint. Add 1¼in (3cm) to this measurement for the seam allowance and this will determine the length of each loop.

4 To decide how many loops you will require, with the needlepoint right side up, place markers such as pins ¼in (5mm) from each side plus half the width of your loop and space markers within those two points. This will be the centre point for each loop. The loops should be far enough apart so as not to distract from the design, but close enough together to support the weight without sagging.

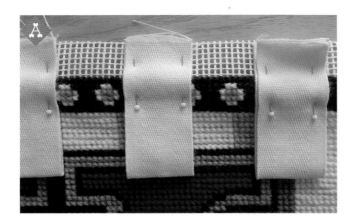

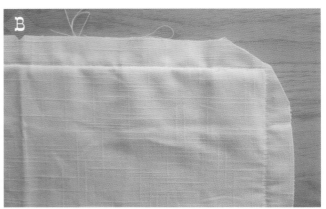

5 Loops can be made from cut ribbon, cut webbing or fabric. If you want to use fabric, take a long length twice the width you require for your finished loops plus an extra 1¼in (3cm). With the right sides of the fabric together, fold to form a long strip and sew down the long raw edges with a seam allowance of ⅝in (1.5cm). Turn the right side out, press and then cut into lengths to form the loops.

6 Working on a flat surface, fold each loop in half and centre over your markers with the raw edges of the loops and the canvas aligned. Attach through all layers with a pin either side of each loop, points facing towards the top edge (◆A).

7 With right sides together, place the lining fabric over your needlepoint and pin all round, marking an opening along the bottom edge wide enough to turn the wall hanging right side out. Machine or **back stitch** (see 'Stitch Glossary', page 26) the layers together with a ⅝in (1.5cm) seam, leaving this gap open.

8 Clip the corner diagonally, avoiding the stitching (◆B). Turn the wall hanging the right side out and press on the backing fabric with a steam iron on wool setting. Turn in the seam allowance of the gap and **slip stitch** (see 'Stitch Glossary' on page 28) closed.

9 Insert the rod or baton through the hoops and tie a length of ribbon or cord to either end to hang. If you find the ribbon or cord slips off the ends of your rod, clear rubber bands around the ends of the rod are perfect for keeping it in place (◆C).

Make it your own!

If you want to increase the size of the wall hanging, work the design in cross stitch using a smaller hole count.

✱ ✱ ✱

FURTHER READING

Anscombe, I., *Arts and Crafts Style*, Phaidon Press, 1996

Barden, B., *The Embroidery Stitch Bible*, Quarto, 2003

Brown, M., *Goldwork Embroidery*, Sally Milner Publishing Pty Ltd, 2007

Carter, J., *New Canvaswork*, Batsford, 2007

Chamberlain, R., *The Beginner's Guide to Goldwork*, Search Press, 2006

Dove, S., *Painting with Stitches*, David Porteous, 2004

Franklin, T., *New Ideas in Goldwork*, Batsford, 2007

Salter, F., *The Bargello Book*, A. & C. Black, 2006

Samuels, C., *Art Deco Textiles*, V&A, 2003

Saunders, S., *Royal School of Needlework Embroidery Techniques*, Batsford, 1998

Sherwood, S., *Contemporary Botanical Artists*, Weidenfeld & Nicolson in association with the Royal Botanic Gardens, Kew, 1996

Springall, D., *Inspired to Stitch*, A. & C. Black, 2005

Synge, L., *Art of Embroidery*, Antique Collectors' Club, 2001

Paine, S., *Embroidered Textiles*, Thames & Hudson, 1990

Pipes, A., *Foundations of Art & Design*, Laurence King, 2008

Rutherford, E., *Silhouette*, Rizzoli, 2009

Waterhouse, J., *Indie Craft*, Laurence King, 2004

SUPPLIERS

If a full postal address is not provided, the supplier is either an online store or there are multiple store locations. Please check the websites for further information.

AUSTRALIA

All Threads Embroidery
Tel: +61 (0)7 3398 5540
www.allthreads.com.au

Australian Craft Network
Tel: +61 (0)2 9682 4418
www.auscraftnet.com.au

Colour Streams
Tel: +61 (0)2 6684 2577
www.colourstreams.com.au

Country Bumpkin
Tel: +61 (0)8 8293 8600
www.countrybumpkin.com.au

Embroidery Source
Tel: +61 (0)3 9499 9492
www.embroiderysource.com.au

J. Leutenegger Pty. Ltd
Tel: +61 (0)2 9256 9200
www.leutenegger.com.au

Punch with Judy
Tel: +61 (0)2 6920 2238
www.punchwithjudy.com.au

Status Thimble
Tel: +61 (0)2 9686 8108
www.statusthimble.com

Stitchers Corner
34 Mint St, East Victoria Park, 6101
Tel: +61 (0)8 9361 4567
www.stitcherscorner.com.au

CANADA

Buttoned Up
614 View St, Victoria, BC, V8W 1J4
Tel: +1 250 384 8781
www.buttonedup.com

Cansew
Tel: +1 514 382 2807
www.cansew.com

Golden Threads Imports Inc.
www.gthreads.com

P and G Enterprises
Tel: +1 877 986 8931
www.pandgenterprises.com

Tanja Berlin
Tel: +1 403 274 6293
www.berlinembroidery.com

UK

Appleton Brothers Ltd
Thames Works, Church St,
Chiswick, London, W4 2PE
Tel: +44 (0)20 8994 0711
www.embroiderywool.co.uk

Creative Beadcraft
Tel: +44 (0)1494 778818
www.creativebeadcraft.co.uk

Creative Quilting
The Specialist Patchwork and Quilting Shop
32 Bridge Rd, Hampton Court Village,
East Molesey, Surrey, KT8 9HA
Tel: +44 (0)208 941 7075
www.creativequilting.co.uk

Friar Gate Frames
67 Church Lane, Darley Abbey,
Derby, DE22 1EX
Tel: +44 (0)1332 554744

Golden Threads
www.goldenthreads.co.uk

John Lewis
Tel: +44 (0)8456 049 049
www.johnlewis.com

Kleins
5 Noel St, London, W1F 8GD
+44 (0)20 7437 6162
www.kleins.co.uk

Macculloch & Wallis
25-26 Dering St, London, W1S 1AT
Tel: +44 (0)207 629 0311
www.macculloch-wallis.co.uk

Mace and Nairn
Tel: +44 (0)1604 864869
www.maceandnairn.com

Pearsall's Silks
Tel: +44 (0)292 063 3353
www.pearsallsembroidery.com

Royal School of Needlework
Tel: +44 (0)203 166 6932
www.royal-needlework.org.uk

Sew Essential
Tel: +44 (0)1922 722276
www.sewessential.co.uk

SMP Lace
Tel: +44 (0)1494 876010
www.smplace.co.uk

The London Bead Co.
339 Kentish Town Rd, London, NW5 2TJ
Tel: +44 (0)207 267 9403
www.londonbeadco.co.uk

VV Rouleaux
261 Pavilion Rd, Sloane Square, London, SW1X 0PB
Tel: +44 (0)207 224 5179
www.vvrouleaux.com

Willow Fabrics
Tel: +44 (0)800 056 7811
www.willowfabrics.com

USA

Aaron Brothers Framing
Tel: +1 888 372 6464
www.aaronbrothers.com

Britex
146 Geary St, San Francisco,
California, 94108
Tel: +1 415 392 2910
www.britexfabrics.com

Coats & Clark
Tel: +1 800 648 1479
www.coatsandclark.com

Create for Less
Tel: +1 866 333 4463
www.createforless.com

Joann Fabrics
Tel: +1 888 739 4120
www.joann.com

Michaels
Tel: +1 800 642 4235
www.michaels.com

Needle in a Haystack
1734 Clement Avenue, Alameda,
California, 94501
Tel: +1 877 429 7822
www.needlestack.com

Potpourri Etc
Tel: +1 800 548 6022
www.rose-cottage.com

Zweigart
Tel: +1 732 388 4545 or +1 800-931 4545
www.zweigart.com

* * *

ABOUT THE AUTHORS

Jessica Aldred

JESSICA is a Graduate Apprentice of the Royal School of Needlework. After her training she worked in Production Costume at the Royal Opera House for three years, buying and maintaining the materials used to make the costumes. In 2008, she returned to the Royal School of Needlework as the Education Coordinator. She runs day classes, the RSN's Certificate and Diploma courses in the USA and organizes and represents the school at various exhibitions across the country. She is also the Student Support Officer for the RSN's Degree in Hand Embroidery.

Throughout her career Jessica has remained self-employed, taking on private commissions and teaching embroidery. She is also a volunteer tutor for Fine Cell Work, a registered charity that teaches needlework to prison inmates and sells their products.

Jessica lives on a houseboat on the river Thames, London, UK, which she shares with her boyfriend and three friends. She has just launched her own range of kits, artwork and customized clothing. You can visit her website at **www.jessicaaldred.co.uk**.

Emily Peacock

EMILY can't remember a time when she didn't have a needle in her hand. Heavily influenced by her years working in graphic design, Emily began designing her cross-stitch kits whilst living for four years in south-western France.

Emily sells her designs on her website **www.emilypeacock.com** as well as in Liberty of London. Her designs have featured extensively in the press and her name is associated with the resurgence in popularity of craft in the UK. She has worked with the charity Fine Cell Work, the degree students at The Royal School of Needlework and collaborated with the designer Rob Ryan. In 2010, Emily appeared on the popular television craft series, **Kirstie's Homemade Home**. She lives in Buckinghamshire, UK, with her husband and two daughters.

165

ACKNOWLEDGEMENTS

Jessica would like to thank…

FIRST AND FOREMOST thank you to my mum, dad and sister Kate for their never-ending love and support, none of this would be possible without you.

A huge thank you to all of my wonderful colleagues at the Royal School of Needlework; in particular, Gill Holdsworth and Amanda Ewing – you have both given me so much support and advice and have asked for nothing in return, your generosity knows no bounds. Thank you to my housemates, Zack Tillman and Abi Coyle, for putting up with me and spurring me on, and to my friends, in particular Kate Brier, Katy Peart and Helen Lovett Johnson, for their words of encouragement and for understanding when I couldn't be around. Also thank you to my friend Lucy Barter who has given help and advice all the way from San Francisco.

Thank you to our Publisher, Jonathan Bailey, our Senior Project Editor, Dominique Page, our Managing Art Editor, Gilda Pacitti, our Editor, Robin Pridy, our Designer, Ali Walper, and all of the brilliant staff at GMC Publications for having faith in Emily and I and for all of your support, hard work and patience.

And last but certainly not least, a massive thank you to my boyfriend Ian Robinson who has quietly stood by me throughout this process, knowing when to give me a cuddle or make me laugh. You will never know how much you have helped.

Emily would like to thank…

FIRSTLY I WOULD LIKE to thank my parents, Angela and John, for their passion, eccentricity and their belief in all things beautiful. I would like to thank my sister, Ali, for her belief in me and always being there to cheer me on. A huge thank you to Katie, who is not only my sister, but my amazing assistant. There is no conceivable way I could have run a business and completed this book without you.

Thank you to those great designers, both living and departed, whose work inspires me – most notably Jean Lurçat, Jean Picard le Doux, Alexander Girard, Rob Ryan and Jonathan Adler.

Huge love to my 'chosen family' for their support, humour and friendship, which has been badly needed at times… my darling Janis, Tina, Kate, Natalie, Erica, Cat and Felicity.

Jess, you are so smart and so talented it's almost irritating. Thank you so much for your hard work and for playing left brain to my right brain. I know I have had to lean on you so much more than I wanted to and am full of gratitude.

Thank you so much to Dominique, Jonathan and Gilda at GMC and Robin our Editor. You have all been so wonderful to work with. Thank you for your patience, guidance and encouragement.

Finally, to Team Peacock – Tony, Ruby and Rosa. How do I even begin? My heart is full.

Picture Credits

Styled photographs by Tim Clinch; canvaswork by Emily Peacock; pages 8–9, 32–33, 74–75, 100–101, 128–129 by the contributors detailed in the captions; all other photographs by Jessica Aldred.

INDEX

GMC Publications Ltd

Castle Place, 166 High Street, Lewes, East Sussex, BN7 1XU

United Kingdom

Tel: +44 (0)1273 488005 **Fax:** +44 (0)1273 402866

Website: www.gmcbooks.com

Orders by credit card are accepted